T0197228

MIND MAGIC

BUILDING A FOUNDATION FOR EMOTIONAL WELL-BEING

JANICE McDERMOTT, M.Ed, MSW

BALBOA.PRESS
A DIVISION OF HAY HOUSE

This publication is designed to provide accurate and personal experience information concerning the subject matter covered. It is sold with the understanding that the authors, contributors, or publishers are not engaged in rendering counseling or other professional services. If counseling advice or other expert assistance is required, seek the services of a competent professional person.

The psychological concepts in this text are based on the four theoretical pillars of Gestalt therapy—phenomenology, dialogical relationship, field theory and experimentation.
Suitable for home, school, institution and group use.
Mind Magic Guided Imagery Edition. Printed in the United States of America
Recordings of each imagery lesson in authors' voice are found at www.healingmindnow.com. Use code HM20N.

Balboa Press books may be ordered through booksellers or by contacting:

Balboa Press
A Division of Hay House
1663 Liberty Drive
Bloomington, IN 47403
www.balboapress.com
844-682-1282

Because of the dynamic nature of the Internet, any web addresses or links contained in this book may have changed since publication and may no longer be valid. The views expressed in this work are solely those of the author and do not necessarily reflect the views of the publisher, and the publisher hereby disclaims any responsibility for them.

The author of this book does not dispense medical advice or prescribe the use of any technique as a form of treatment for physical, emotional, or medical problems without the advice of a physician, either directly or indirectly. The intent of the author is only to offer information of a general nature to help you in your quest for emotional and spiritual well-being. In the event you use any of the information in this book for yourself, which is your constitutional right, the author and the publisher assume no responsibility for your actions.

Any people depicted in stock imagery provided by Getty Images are models, and such images are being used for illustrative purposes only.
Certain stock imagery © Getty Images.

Print information available on the last page.

ISBN: 978-1-9822-6753-7 (sc)
ISBN: 978-1-9822-6751-3 (e)

Library of Congress Control Number: 2021907655

Balboa Press rev. date: 05/11/2021

CONTENTS

PHYSICAL NEEDS

SAFETY NEEDS

PSYCHOLOGICAL AND SOCIAL NEEDS

BUILDING SELF-ESTEEM

SELF-ACTUALIZING

PREFACE
PREVIOUS GROUNDWORK

From early childhood until death, mental health is the springboard of thinking and communication skills—learning, emotional growth, resilience, and self-esteem. These are the ingredients of each individual's successful contribution to community and society. Americans are inundated with messages about success—in school, in a profession, in parenting, in relationships—without appreciating that successful performance rests on a foundation of mental health.*

Every child deserves to have these mental health tools necessary to build a stable and productive life. It is from one's own internal strength that good mental health functioning occurs.**

One of the basic tenets of good emotional health is that people must learn to control *what* and *how* they think about the world they live in.

*J. Secker, "Current Conceptualizations of Mental Health and Mental Health Priorities," *Health Education Research*, 13 no. 1, (1998): 57–66.

**Hawkins, Catalano, and Miller, "Risk and protective factors for alcohol and other drug problems in adolescence and early adulthood: Implications for substance abuse prevention." *Psychol. Bull.* 112 no.1 (1992): 64–105.

With this concept in mind, educator Joan Stewart, MSW and I, both practicing licensed clinical social workers in Saint Francisville, Louisiana, developed and implemented a guided imagery mental health pilot project in West Feliciana Middle School, titled Guided Imagery Mental Health Education Project (GIMHE), during the second semester of the 2002–3 school year. Area Health Education Center (AHEC) funded the project through a Better Health for the

Delta grant. McDermott and Stewart worked with twenty-four participants, including special needs participants, regular education participants, and gifted and talented participants, by teaching these participants to manage their emotions and behavior with guided imagery and relaxation techniques. The middle school faculty selected these participants for a variety of reasons—family problems, disruptive behavior, anxiety, depression, or bereavement.

Evaluation

The following evaluation report for *Mind Magic*, formerly called the Grand Ideas from Within (GIFW) program, was completed by Ariel Ngnitedem, PhD, Southern University, Baton Rouge, Louisiana, in 2009. This report is the third in a series of evaluations of the GIFW program.

For the 2008–9 year's study a before and after quasi-experimental design with a single group was used. A sample of seventh-, eighth-, and ninth-grade participants attending Plaquemine High School and five of their teachers were surveyed (before and after the implementation of the GIFW program) regarding participant behavior, attitude, and drug use. Data on attendance, discipline, GPAs, and failing grades of the 312 participants attending Plaquemine High was collected before and after the implementation of the GIFW program as well. Simple statistics (percentages, means, and so forth) were primarily used to *describe* the pre- and post-datasets, and the t-test was used to *compare* the mean scores of the pretests and posttests. The executive summary for the 2008–9 year's study reports significant changes in participants after participating in GIFW:

1. Grade point averages improved
2. Failures in the group room decreased
3. Attendance improved
4. Likelihood of losing their temper decreased
5. Likelihood of finding it difficult to concentrate decreased
6. Likelihood of disapproving of fellow participants using marijuana increased
7. Time period during which participants experienced difficulties with emotions, concentration, behavior, or the ability to get along with other people decreased
8. Number of participants who acknowledged being taught how to mediate, relax, or reduce stress increased

The report gives the following recommendation:

Continue the implementation of this program at the same schools, extend it to other schools in the state of Louisiana, and eventually to other schools in the nation. Mississippi is the second state to use the GIFW program in their public schools. (As of 2012, Mississippi has used the program in five schools.)

"The quality of the future of education depends not on the quantitative expansion of access and availability of education, as is commonly thought, but on a transformation of the way individuals think of themselves as learners, and an awareness that certain mental and emotional prerequisites ("scaffolding") need to be in place before learning can occur. Many children are disenchanted by schools because they have come to see themselves as incapable of handling academic work and feel that the curriculum is not relevant to life outside school. They are not receptive to learning because of the negative perceptions they hold of themselves as individuals and as learners. The questions that need to be asked are not how many subjects can we cram into a school day, but what is the motivation and mental/emotional state of the learner? Can children be taught to shift their capacity to learn?"

—Caroline Mann, PhD, MEd, NLP master practitioner

KINDS OF GUIDED IMAGERY

1. **Feeling State Imagery:** Changes mood. Any imagery that can elicit a delightful feeling and replace doubt, fear, or anxiety.

2. **End-State Imagery:** Uses for its content any desired outcome or goal.

3. **Energetic Imagery:** Any image that generates an internal feeling of motion or the movement of time.

4. **Cellular Imagery:** Uses accurate medical information but focuses on the healthy interaction of cells.

5. **Physiological Imagery:** Similar to cellular imagery only larger in scope, such as imagining the shrinking of a tumor.

6. **Psychological Imagery:** Built around real-life issues, such as walking through your recently destroyed home to cope with the loss.

7. **Metaphoric Imagery:** Uses symbols in place of reality, such as the planting of a seed as a symbol of dying.

8. **Spiritual Imagery:** Includes religious or spiritual references such as hearing the voice of God in the wind, creates a sense of oneness, transcendence.

INTRODUCTION

The mind is always in a constant process of creating something. It never stops. In an interview in 1929 with a *Post* reporter Albert Einstein said, "Imagination is more important than knowledge." (Saturdayeveningpost.com). We would like to add that it is an essential component of good mental health. Without direction, the mind wanders and we daydream. When we take time to notice, we give ourselves the opportunity to direct our minds' powerful energy.

From time to time, we daydream to feel happy or to entertain ourselves by making up future life episodes. On other occasions, we re-create the past—the way it was or the way we wish it could have been—and feel sad.

Everything—the chair we sit on, the tires on our car, and the robbery we read about in the paper—was first dreamed up in someone's mind, with intention or not. Every manufactured creation in our environment first appeared in someone's imagination. What are you imagining right now in the background of your mind?

There are endless possibilities when we are responsible imaginers. Responsibility produces intended outcomes—desired results. We can solve problems, build better relationships, create success, and strengthen our confidence. Intended group imagining, imagining the same outcome together, creates a better life and world for all!

Our imaginations engage all of our five senses—sight, hearing, body sensations, taste, and smell. What we imagine stirs our emotions as well. We feel glad, mad, sad, and sometimes afraid. Children under eight often scare themselves with their own creative imagining of monsters under the bed.

When anticipating a joyful event, we often feel excitement run through our bodies—so grand at times that it spills out of our bodies and passes through our *excitement threshold* into anxiety. This process occurs especially when we follow our imagined joyful event with an image of something interfering with it.

We may imagine the voice of a parent saying, "Now don't get too excited." What does *too excited* mean? As children, we make up what it means—"Something bad is going to happen"—and scare ourselves with what we hear or see in our imaginations.

What did you imagine as a child that made you afraid of your own excitement? Whatever it was, you may notice that you continue to play the image every time you begin to get very excited and then you get anxious.

Is your imagination leading you in all directions? Take charge of the images in your mind. Bad choices limit future options.

IBM once ran a three-page advertisement as early as 2003, Volume 25, issue 11, of the *Inc. 500* business magazine. On each page appeared a person with eyes closed and the caption "Can you see it?" This suggests that IBM is busy imagining, dreaming, making faster decisions, lowering costs, and having better collaborations, better systems delivery, and better services. Certainly, IBM is actively implying that to improve output, we must first imagine the outcome.

Michael Joseph, founder and president of the nonprofit Joseph and Edna Josephson Institute of Ethics, believes "We can't insulate children from all negative experiences—pressure to succeed, self-doubt, or feelings of alienation. However, we can help them develop emotional resilience, the inner strength to purge themselves of toxic feelings, rather than just suck it up and move on. We can teach kids how to lose without being defeated, how to fail and not become failures, and how to deal with rejection without becoming hopelessly dejected. We also need to teach kids to be realistically optimistic, to believe absolutely in the capacity to survive, to trust that 'This too shall pass,' and truly believe that better days are ahead. We can teach them Little Orphan Annie's undaunted confidence that no matter how dark it is today, 'the sun will come out tomorrow.'

The guided imagery activities provided here in *Mind Magic* are original to the group room edition of Grand Ideas from Within. They provide the tools necessary for focusing our imaginations on desired goal outcomes while at the same time developing mental health skills. Guided imagery, with you or someone else as the guide, is a universal path to the subconscious mind. Essentially, it frees us from distractions and fears, and it convinces our conscious selves of our goals. It is a way to help us hear what our intuition is saying from our between state of waking and sleeping.

In this relaxed state, the inner mind allows us to heed our own suggestions and concentrate on messages we put there. Negative statements from the unconscious mind or silent voice become inactive. In this state, we impress ourselves with what we say.

It is important to allow adequate time for immersion into our internal selves and the imagery process. When an image emerges, allow it to speak to you rather than forcing a meaning. Focus on dynamics and process rather than content.

When sharing images with another person, it is important to use first-person present-tense language, to hear it aloud as though it were happening now—for example, "I *am* walking down a yellow brick road" rather than "I was walking." Share your image even when your understanding is not clear. Meaning often evolves from sharing.

Choose interpretations that validate both internal and external realities. Acknowledge the areas of resonance, which give validity to your own and others' experience. Avoid over-questioning the content of an image or focusing on history that is not relevant to current happenings. Avoid selective omission due to fears or beliefs and save moral judgments for a different conversation. By practicing these guided imagery exercises, all can begin to create a more productive way of life.

GOALS, OBJECTIVES, PERFORMANCE

Goals

➢ To support positive qualities typical of children age ten through adulthood
➢ To enhance language processing skills
➢ To improve mental health functioning
➢ To build resilience for coping and decision making

Objectives

A. Participants will gain awareness of internal resources available for success
B. Participants will strengthen four specific qualities vital to achieving success:
   1. Internal processes for handling frustration, anxiety, and depression
   2. Tolerance for delayed gratification
   3. Self-confidence (strengthened self-esteem)
   4. Positive ideals and future aspirations

Performance Indicators

A. Fewer discipline problems
B. Regular attendance
C. Better academic/skill performance
D. Positive attitude toward nonuse of drugs and alcohol
E. Interest in coeducational activities
F. Desiring adult leadership roles and autonomy in planning
G. Demonstrates community consciousness
H. Seeks opportunities for self-expression
I. Expresses needs of self and understands the needs of others
J. Displays resilience for coping and decision making

Imagery is one of those things we teach people because we really do believe that doing that kind of thinking increases the potential and probability for performing well.

—Jim Bowen, Olympic training on-site psychologist

LEADER GUIDELINES

Group Leader: Counselor, Parent, Tutor

1. Follow lessons 1–8 in sequence. The remaining lessons may vary to fit the situation.
2. An important component of the imagery process is playing relaxing music to set the tone for the exercise as participants take their seats.
3. Read and discuss the "Purpose and Overview" of each lesson with participants and explain any handouts or exercises.
4. Display each lesson's quote for further discussion and insight. The quote enhances the lesson, exposes participants to a wide variety of authors and literature, and provides an opportunity for further study.
5. Keep paper and writing or drawing materials readily available. Journaling and drawing exercises help participants process and implement imagery. (Reviewing worksheets or journals and providing a verbal or tangible reward for *any* entry will increase performance and success. Any entry is acceptable. It is important not to judge a participant's process. If a participant is making important or exceptional entries, increase the reward. A group or home privilege rather than a purchased item is the preferred reward. Be creative and engage the participants in determining session rewards.
6. Use the same calm, soothing voice and rhythmic pace when reading an imagery exercise. Pause to the count of five for three dots (…), the count of ten with the word *pause*, and the count of fifteen for a *long pause*. An asterisk at the beginning of a particular day's imagery exercise indicates the script to use for the once-a-week group presentation for that lesson.
7. Allow adequate time for participants to relax into the imagery process. You will notice a slower rate of breathing, less body movement, and a change in affect (similar to sleep).
8. Encourage participants by saying one or more of the following:
   - Allow an image to form, or to speak to you, rather than consciously forcing a meaning.
   - Follow the narrator's voice and go where it takes you—if you wander off, simply return to the sound of the narrator's voice or go with the flow.
   - Share an image even when your understanding is not clear. Don't hold back images due to fears or beliefs.
   - Use first-person present-tense language when sharing images—speak and hear it as though it is happening now.
   - Acknowledge and validate each other's experience without questioning content or giving advice.

9. Support individual's interpretation of images or exercises that validate each individual's internal (perceptual) and external (actual) reality. Save moral judgments for a different discussion.

10. Know that bullying often occurs because of an unexpressed emotion such as grief or anger. Lessons 3 and 8 apply to the person bullied, who learns to feel separate from the identity of the victim self. In lessons 11–14, the bully develops more self-compassion and responsibility and hence is less likely to act out.

An Answer to Violence

"Our bodies carry the potential for self-knowledge, self-healing, love, and compassion. By reawakening our perceptive skills of feeling, sensing and initiating, we allow the wisdom of the body to emerge, to guide and inform us. Peace begins where we live—in our bodies. By working sincerely and directly with our present body-felt condition, we can begin to affect our life as well as the lives of others. When we heal our self, we heal others."

—Janice McDermott, MEd, LCSW. 2015. *Healing Mind, Five Steps to Ultimate Healing, Four Rooms for Thoughts: Achieving Satisfaction through a Well-Managed Mind*

COMMON CORE STANDARDS ADDRESSED

Language Arts and Literacy in History/Social Studies
Lesson 1
- *Speaking and listening:* for example, speaking intelligibly
- *Reasoning skills:* for example, cause/effect, generating inquiry, connecting to real-life situations

Lesson 2
- *Reasoning skills:* for example, cause/effect, connecting to real-life situations

Lesson 3
- *Make use of information:* for example, summarizing
- *Reasoning skills:* for example, facts/opinions

Lessons 4–7
- *Reasoning skills:* for example, facts/opinions

Lesson 8
- *Write competently:* for example, texts and life experiences
- *Speaking and listening:* for example, group discussion
- *Reasoning skills:* for example, fact/opinion, cause/effect, generating inquiry, connect to real-life situations

Lesson 9
- *Read, comprehend, and respond:* for example, connect to real-life situations

Lesson 10
- *Write competently:* for example, texts and life experiences

Lesson 11, 12, 13
- *Write competently:* for example, texts and life experiences
- *Speaking and listening:* for example, group discussions

- *Locate, select, and make use of information*: for example, summarizing
- *Reasoning skills:* for example, fact/ opinion, cause/effect, generating inquiry, connect to real-life situations

Lesson 14
- *Reasoning skills:* for example, comprehension strategies, cause/effect, generating inquiry, connect to real-life situations
- *Speaking and listening:* for example, group discussions, connect to real-life situations

Lessons 15–17
- Write competently: for example, texts and life experiences
- *Reasoning skills:* for example, inductive/deductive reasoning, comprehension strategies, cause/effect, generating inquiry, connect to real-life situations

EMOTIONAL WELL-BEING SKILLS

Lessons

1. Managing the Body
   - Self-awareness and control
   - Stress management
2. Learning to Breathe
   - Self-awareness and control
   - Stress management
3. Foreground and Background
   - Acceptance, open-mindedness, cooperation, tolerance
   - Adaptability, compassion, relationship building
   - Peer relations, fairness, nonviolence
   - Conflict resolution (antibullying)
   - Self-awareness, stress-management
4. Seeing What I See
   - Visual awareness, creativity imagining
   - Success building
5. Hearing What I Hear
   - Developing auditory images to support oral and written communication
6. Sensing Outer Space
   - Heightening awareness of body sensation
7. Smelling and Tasting
   - Awakening awareness to how smell and taste can influence our choices and changes in our behaviors
8. Feeling Safe
   - Building internal strength, self-discipline, courage
   - Adaptability, coping strategy
9. Shifting Perception: Shifting Emotions
   - Conflict resolution (bullying), nonviolence, peer relations
   - Self-esteem building, identifying and controlling emotions
     - Glad (happy)
     - Mad (anger)
     - Sad (bereavement, depression)

- ○ Afraid (anxiety)
10. Anchoring with Transitional Objects
    - Adaptability, confidence, anxiety reduction
    - Perseverance, self-motivation, accessing mental information
11. Exploring My World
    - Appreciation, positive attitude, play
12. Mending What's Broken
    - Self-acceptance, patience
    - Positive thinking and attitude
13. Managing My Mind
    - Internal responsibility, free will
    - Self-esteem building, organized thinking
14. Building Self Esteem
    - Positive thanking,
    - Recognizing personal attributes
15. Accepting Myself and Others
    - Compassion, courage
    - Responsibility, self-acceptance
    - Self-respect, better choices
16. Praising Self and Others
    - Positive expression, self-praise, peer relationships, oral communication
17. Winds of Change
    - Initiative, self-direction, responsibility
    - Open-mindedness, self-confidence
    - Perseverance, creating positive change
18. Creating Success
    - Broadening possibilities, goal setting, self-direction, self-confidence
    - Better choices, perseverance, open-mindedness
    - Responsibility, industriousness, positive change
19. Bridges to the Future
    - Broadening possibilities, goal setting, self-direction, self-confidence
    - Better choices, perseverance, open-mindedness
    - Responsibility, industrious, positive change

CLIMBING MASLOW'S LADDER OF HUMAN NEEDS

(6) Self-transcendence—becoming more than the self, more than the body

(5) Self-actualizing—become all of what one is capable of becoming

(4) Self-esteem—feeling good about yourself, internal nurturing

(3) Psychological and social needs—acceptance, belonging, love

(2) Safety needs—security, stability

(1) Physical needs—air, water, food, shelter, sex

PHYSICAL NEEDS

AIR, WATER, FOOD, SEX

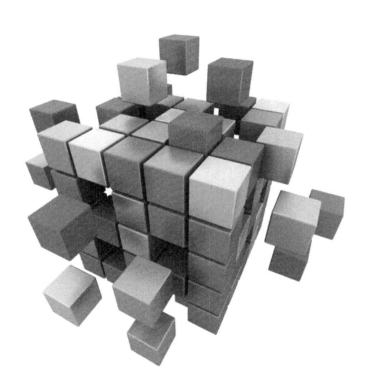

MANAGING MY BODY

This body, full of faults, has yet one great quality: whatever it encounters in this temporal life depends upon one's actions.

—Ralph Waldo Emerson

Lesson 1: Self-Control

Grade Level: 2–12

Purpose and Overview: Our muscles hold accumulated stress-induced tension, the result of daily hassles—noise, poor lighting, too little space, too many rules, boring activities, and unpleasant people. In the first stage of stress, the body responds with panic, a fight-or-flight reaction—our hormones increase, our hearts beat faster, we breathe harder, we sweat, our senses are more alert, and we prepare to protect ourselves by running or attacking. Most of the time, the running is inside ourselves, as is the verbal attack that produces a physical response of fear, anxiety, panic, anger, or the need to cry. We also lose some of our mental alertness and internal organization in this process.

Individuals in a public speaking situation are quite often familiar with this response. Before speaking, their hearts beat faster, their mouths get drier, and they get confused. Some may even get nauseated or feel faint. They may shake as their bodies urge them to run rather than speak. Their voices may tremble. We work to resist this state of alarm, adjust to the stressor, and try to calm down. Even when we are successful, the body is still tense as it works to become more accustomed to the stress. However, in this process, our concentration and decision-making continue to be poor. The longer the stress, the more our immune systems weaken, until we become ill.

When it is impossible to flee the stressor—such as a teacher, parent, or boss looking over our shoulders day after day—we can learn new ways to bring our bodies' automatic responses under control. We can relieve the stress and tension that interfere with individual optimum performance through techniques of relaxation and imagery.

In 1939, Edmund Jacobson developed the progressive muscular relaxation technique to relax our muscles in order to reduce stress. The process includes tightening a muscle to extreme tension, holding for a few seconds, and then relaxing the muscle to its previous state. Finally, the focus turns to relaxing the muscle even further to make it as relaxed as possible. The technique is similar to the idea of a swinging clock pendulum or a playground swing—if you want something to swing in a particular direction, then you must first pull it in the opposite direction and let go.

The process consists of working systematically through the body, starting with the hands, working up to the shoulders, and then working from the feet to the shoulders again. The face and neck are last. It is of utmost importance to coordinate breathing with the tension/relaxation cycle. Every time you release the tightened muscles, exhale and feel the tension go out from the selected muscle group along with the outgoing breath. The breathing must be relaxed and preferably come from the abdomen.

Objective: Participants will be able to calm themselves through noticing their bodies' responses and relaxing when in stressful situations such as oral presentations, test taking, conflict, or the presence of authority.

Materials Needed:
1. Daily imagery scripts and calm instrumental music to play in background.
2. Weekly recordings: Grand Ideas from Within Counselor Edition: Audio-Guided Imagery, Volume 1, track 1, "Relax My Body A" (5:40); track 2, "Relax My Body B" (4:09); track 10, "Background Music."
3. Display week's title and quote.

Note: With younger participants, introduce the word *buttocks* before the exercise begins to prevent giggles during the guided imagery. Encourage participants with physical disabilities to imagine their body is working as suggested—for example, imagine standing when actually unable to do so.

Present Lesson Overview:
Read designated daily imagery script with background music of choice or play weekly audio imagery activity, Volume 1, track 1, "Relax My Body A."

Note: Days 1 and 2 may be combined.

Day 1: This exercise is the first half of the process for progressive muscular relaxation. When physically possible, participants stand by the right side of their chair with Grand Ideas from Within Counselor Edition, Volume 1, track 10, "Background Music" playing. If group is once a week, combine days 1, 2, and 3.

Imagery Script:
First Half of Muscle Relaxation
1. Say, "Do not speak until directed. As you breathe in and out through your nose, allow my voice to guide you. You know you have complete control over your imagination and are free to go wherever you like within your own mind. Look straight ahead at a spot on the wall. Pretend you have an orange or a wet sponge in each hand, and now squeeze it as tight as you can and hold it. Now relax your hand as you release the orange or sponge, allowing it to fall to the floor. Relax your hand even more." Pause.

2. "While looking at the spot on the wall, notice your arms. Tighten your biceps and lower arms together, as tight as you can." Pause. "And then release and relax them even more. Now, as you continue to look at the spot, focus on your shoulders. Inhale, hold your breath, and raise your shoulders as if to touch your ears; hold and exhale, letting your shoulders fall, relaxed even more. While looking at the wall, think of your feet. Breathing in, curl up your toes; hold and release on your exhale."

3. "Noticing the front of your legs, breathing in, point your foot away from you so that it is almost parallel with your leg, like that of a ballet dancer. Hold and release—and now the other foot. Breathing in, point your foot away from you, hold, and release on the exhale."

4. "Breathing in through your nose, flex your feet upward, heels down, stretching the backs of your legs. Hold, release, and relax on the exhale. Now close your eyes and tighten your whole body—tight, tighter, tighter—and release on the exhale, bending forward, almost touching your toes, and shaking all over: shake, shake, shake, stop. Breathe deeply and be seated. You may speak to the group."

Day 2: This exercise is the second half of the process for progressive muscular relaxation. Participants remain seated with background music playing.

Note: Younger participants may imagine they are the only ones with their eyes closed and laugh or peek while closing their eyes. To manage this, have participants sit in a circle facing outward, with their backs toward the center, until they get comfortable with having closed eyes. Comment, "Everyone has their eyes closed—wonderful!" Repeat until everyone is settled with eyes closed. Everyone should be comfortable by the end of this exercise.

Imagery Script:
Second Half of "Relax My Body"

1. Say, "Do not speak until directed. Look straight ahead at a spot on the wall. We are going to utilize the second half of the process for progressive muscular relaxation. Put your hands in your lap and close your mouth, breathing through your nose. Feel your thighs tighten under your hands. Tighten them more, hold, and release as you breathe out. Raise your feet off the floor, lifting your knees as high as you can where you are sitting, holding, and breathing out, lowering your feet to the floor, and relaxing your thighs even more."

2. "Breathing in, clench your buttocks together. Hold, release, and relax. Hold your stomach muscles in tight, tighter; release with a sigh and relax them even more." Pause.

3. "Breathing in, press the small of your back against the chair, and hold. Breathing out, release and relax." Pause.

4. "Breathing in, hold your breath and tighten all your chest muscles. Hold, breathe out, release, and relax." Pause.

5. "Breathing in, hold your breath and raise your shoulders as if to touch your ears. Hold, releasing as you exhale." Pause.

6. "Inhaling, stretch your head up, as if your chin could touch the ceiling, and exhale as you lower your head until your chin reaches your neck … relax." Pause.

7. "Press your lips together and clench your teeth."

8. "Squeeze your eyes shut … tighter. Open your eyes and raise your eyebrows as high as you can, as if they could disappear over the back of your head; hold and release."

9. "Tighten up all the muscles in your face; hold and release. Now breathe deeply." Pause. "You may speak to the group."

Day 3: This exercise is the complete process for progressive muscular relaxation. Participants remain seated with relaxing music playing in the background. Play audio Grand Ideas from Within Counselor Edition, Volume 1, track 1, "Relax My Body A," or read script with background music of choice.

Imagery Script:
Complete Relaxing Process
"Background Music," Volume 1, track 10

1. Say, "Do not speak until directed. Look straight ahead at a spot on the wall. Using the progressive muscular relaxation process, pretend you have an orange in each hand, squeeze it as tight as you can, and hold it. Relax your hands as you release the oranges, allowing them to fall to the floor. Relax your hand even more." Pause.

2. "While looking at the spot on the wall, notice your arms. Tighten your biceps and lower arms, together, without the hands, as tight as you can." Pause. "And then release and relax them even more."

3. "Now, as you continue to look at the spot, focus on your shoulders. Inhale, hold your breath, raise your shoulders as if to touch your ears, and hold." Pause. "Exhale, letting your shoulders fall, relaxed even more. While looking at the wall, think of your feet. Breathing in, curl up your toes and hold. Release on your exhale."

4. "Notice the fronts of your legs. Breathing in, point your right foot away from you so that it is almost parallel with your leg, like that of a ballet dancer. Hold … and release—and now the other foot. Breathing in, point your foot away from you and hold. Pause. "Release on the exhale."

5. "Breathing in through your nose, flex your feet upward, heels down, stretching the backs of your legs. Hold, release, and relax on the exhale."

6. "Put your hands in your lap and close your mouth, breathing through your nose. Feel your thighs tighten under your hands. Tighten them more, hold … and release as you breathe out. Raise your feet off the floor, lifting your knees as high as you can from where you are sitting. Hold, breathing out, lowering your feet to the floor, relaxing your thighs even more."

7. "Breathing in, clench your buttocks together and hold. Release and relax. Hold your stomach muscles in tight, tighter, release with a sigh, and relax them even more." Pause.

8. "Breathing in, press the small of your back against the chair and hold. Breathing out, release and relax." Pause.

9. "Breathing in, hold your breath and tighten all your chest muscles. Hold. Breathe out, release, and relax." Pause.

10. "Breathing in, hold your breath and raise your shoulders as if to touch your ears. Hold, releasing as you exhale." Pause.

11. "Inhaling, stretch your head up, as if your chin can touch the ceiling, and exhale moving your head forward until your chin reaches your chest, and relax." Pause.

12. "Press your lips together and clench your teeth. Squeeze your eyes shut, tighter. Open your eyes and raise your eyebrows as high as you can, as if they can disappear over the back of your head. Hold and then release." Pause.

13. "Tense up all the muscles in your face. Hold and release. Now breathe deeply. You may speak to the group."

Day 4: This exercise repeats the complete process for progressive muscular relaxation with only a few words of guidance, and it suggests that participants keep their eyes closed for the complete exercise. Participants remain seated with relaxing music playing in the background. Play audio Grand Ideas from Within Counselor Edition, Volume 1, track 2, "Relax My Body B" or read script.

Imagery Script:

Relax My Body
Volume 1, track 2, "Relax My Body B"

1. Say, "Look straight ahead at a spot on the wall. Now close your eyes. With eyes closed, imagine you are seeing the spot on the wall." Pause. "Now turn your attention toward your body, keeping your eyes closed. This time notice the difference in your breathing when you tense and when you relax. I am only going to give you a reminder. For each body part that I mention, I want you to locate it, breathe in as you tighten it, hold the tension, and breathe out as you release it."

2. "Starting with hands, begin; imagine holding an orange in each hand and then squeeze, hold, and release."

3. "Squeeze Arms and shoulders, inhale; hold your breath and raise your shoulders as if to touch your ears. Hold, tighter, and release with the exhale."

4. "Feet … front of legs, point your foot away from you." Pause. "Back of legs: flex your feet upward and stretch your heels away from your body." Long pause. "Thighs." Long pause. "Bottom: clench your buttocks together and hold." Pause. "Release and relax." Pause.

5. "Stomach: hold your stomach muscles in tight, tighter, and release." Pause.

6. "Press the small of your back against the chair." Pause. "Release on your exhale."

7. "Chest: breathe in, hold your breath, and tighten all your chest muscles." Pause. "And release."

8. "Shoulders: breathe in, hold your breath, and raise your shoulders as if to touch your ears." Pause until shoulders fall.

9. "Neck: chin stretches to the ceiling. Hold and then breathe out as your chin presses into your chest." Pause.
10. "Mouth and jaw: press your lips together and clench your teeth. Release." Pause.
11. "Close eyes tighter and, keeping your eyes closed, release."
12. "Raise your eyebrows as if they could disappear over your head." Pause. "And now your face … and relaxing all over." Pause.
13. "Open your eyes and breathe deeply. You may speak to the group."

Note: Do not judge experiences—simply acknowledge that each is a unique experience.

Day 5: This exercise is an accumulation of the previous ones. The participants remain seated with relaxing music playing in the background.

1. Say, "Do not speak until directed. Close your eyes. Now, with eyes closed, I will only give a few reminders for progressive muscle relaxation. You will follow the process from your previous day's practice. Beginning with your hands, remember the oranges and tighten your fist." Pause. "Arms, without the hands." Pause.
2. "Shoulders: inhale and raise your shoulders as if to touch your ears." Pause. "Feet: curl up your toes." Pause. "Front of legs: point your foot." Pause Back of legs: flex your feet upward." Pause. "Thighs: lift feet." Pause.
3. "Bottom: clench your buttocks together." Pause. "Stomach: tight, tighter." Pause. "Lower back: press the small of your back into the chair." Pause.
4. "Chest: inhale and tighten all your chest muscles." Pause. "Shoulders again to ears." Pause.
5. "Neck: inhale with chin up … and exhale with chin down." Pause. "Mouth and jaw: press your lips together and clench your teeth." Pause. "Eyes: close tighter." Pause.
6. "Forehead: raise your eyebrows." Pause.
7. "Face: tighten all the muscles up together." Pause. "Imagine all your tension is evaporating into thin air as you become perfectly relaxed, with nowhere to go and nothing to do for a whole minute—all the time in the world." Pause for one minute.
8. "Slowly open your eyes and breathe deeply." Pause. "You may speak to the group."

Note: Do not judge experiences—simply acknowledge each as a unique experience.

Verification of Participants' Understanding: Notice the participants' physical responses— their tightening and releasing of muscles and following directions. Their affect will also change as they become more relaxed and quiet. When eyes are closed, tension leaves their faces and they appear peaceful as if sleeping. Ask a volunteer to repeat orally the steps in the relaxing process, beginning with the breath.

Reinforce with Independent Activity: Encourage those who are self-conscious. Ask participants to engage in stress-reducing muscle tensing and relaxing when in a long sitting exercise, such as writing or test taking, and invite them to share their experiences with you from time to time.

Other Resources:
Jacobson, Edmund. 1993. *Progressive Relaxation.* Chicago: University of Chicago Press.

Additional Notes:

LEARNING TO BREATHE

Breathe in experience, breathe out poetry.

—Muriel Rukeyser

Lesson 2: Self-control through breathing (incorporates the *relaxation response* material introduced in lesson 1)

Grade Level: 2–12

Purpose and Overview: Learning to use the breath resourcefully can play a major role in reducing stress and creating the sense of confidence needed to meet challenging situations. A lifetime of fear-based shallow breathing patterns can be unlearned, clearing the way for natural, free, unrestricted breathing that energizes every aspect of life.

The average person breathes approximately 21,600 times per day. The in breath delivers over eighty-eight pounds of oxygen to the bloodstream, which circulates the most important nutrient in the body to each cell. The exhale then plays the vital role of removing 70 percent of the waste products from the body. In addition, breathing links the body and mind, the conscious and subconscious.

Inefficient upper chest breathing leaves the body oxygen-starved, thereby increasing the respiration rate in an effort to catch more breath. Without enough oxygen, we are breathless and our brains operate less efficiently. Shallow breathing patterns trigger the stress response cycle (similar to a fear response) within the sympathetic nervous system, which transmits more stress signals to the breathing mechanism. However, with training in breath awareness and special breathing techniques, we can begin to bring our breathing patterns out of our unconscious and into our conscious control. Harvard Medical School tested the technique used in this writing, described in *The Relaxation Response,* by Dr. Herbert Benson.

When we are relaxed enough, we can heed our own suggestions and affirmations. The use of metaphors, a technique of guided imagery, can anchor images, enhance memory, and aid review of materials.

Note: This week's lesson can be conducted as an exercise before an important meeting, an exam, homework, family meal time, or bedtime.

Objective: Participants will be able to calm themselves through proper breathing when in stressful situations or when experiencing anxiety.

Materials Needed:
1. Imagery script or recording Grand Ideas from Within Counselor Edition: Audio-Guided Imagery, Volume 1, track 2, "Relax My Body B" (4:09); track 3 "Take a Deep Breath" (4:39)
2. Display lesson's title and quote

Present Lesson Overview:
Read imagery script or listen to audio Grand Ideas from Within Counselor Edition, Volume 1, track 2, "Relax My Body (B)"; track 3, "Take a Deep Breath."

Imagery Script:

Learning to Breathe

Days 1 and 2: Begin with relaxing music in the background. Participants remain seated.

Say, "Do not speak until directed. Look straight ahead at a spot on the wall. Pay attention to your breathing." Pause.

1. "Let us begin by calming the body." Wait for the group to become still. "Close your eyes." Pause. "And begin to breathe quietly through your nose." Pause. "Again, notice your breathing." Pause.
2. "As you breathe out through your nose, silently, to yourself, say the word *one*." Pace with the rhythm of group's breathing.
3. "Breathe in ... out, *one*. In ... out, *one*. In ... out, *one*. In ... out, *one*. Now, breathing easily and naturally, sit quietly at first with your eyes closed." Wait ten seconds. "And sit quietly with your eyes open." Wait ten seconds. "You may speak to the group. What did you notice?"

Days 3–5: Participants remain seated with relaxing music playing in the background.

Read imagery script with background music or play audio, Volume 1, track 3, "Take a Deep Breath."

Imagery Script:

Take a Deep Breath

1. Say, "Do not speak until directed. Look straight ahead at a spot on the wall. Pay attention to your breathing." Continue slowly with a calm voice.

2. "Now let us begin by calming the body." Wait for group to become still. "Close your eyes." Pause. "And begin to breathe quietly through your nose." Pause. "Just notice your breathing." Pause. "As you breathe out through your nose, silently, to yourself, say the word *one* (pace with the rhythm of group's breathing). Breathe in … out, *one*. In … out, *one*. In … out, *one*. In … out, *one*. As your breathing finds its rhythm, notice how calm and relaxed you can become. Now become more relaxed." Pause. "Becoming ever calmer and more relaxed, continue to breathe while silently saying the word *one*." Pause. "No place to go and nothing to do for the next minute." Pause for one minute. "Now bring your attention back to your body." Pause. "And now back to the room." Pause.

3. "Breathing easily and naturally, sit quietly at first with your eyes closed." Pause for ten seconds. "And now sit quietly with your eyes open." Pause for ten seconds. "Each of your experiences is unique and valuable. What did you notice? You may speak to the group." Pause. "How are you different?"

Verification of Participants' Understanding: (1) Notice changes in affect and the rise and fall of participants' chests when directed to breathe in and out. (2) Ask participants to describe the difference between regular breathing and stress-reduction breathing. (3) Ask participants to journal—write about experiences or verbally describe them.

Note: Do not judge experience; acknowledge that everyone has his or her own unique valuable experience.

Reinforce with Independent Activity: Ask participants to engage in stress-reduction breathing prior to trying something new or when frustrated, such as when test taking, presenting an oral report, or participating in a competition.

Other Resources:

Benson, Herbert. 1990. *The Relaxation Response.* New York: Harper Mass Market.

Khalsa, Gurcharan Singh, and Yogi Bhajan. 2000. *Breath Walk: Breathing Your Way to a Revitalized Body, Mind, and Spirit.* New York: Broadway Books.

Additional Notes:

FOREGROUND AND BACKGROUND

> Disability is a matter of perception. If you can do just one thing well,
> you're needed by someone.
>
> —Martina Navratilova

Lesson 3: Shifting Perceptions

Grade Level: 4–12

Purpose and Overview: Webster defines perception as *a mental image, concept, awareness of the elements of the environment through physical sensation,* and as *physical sensation interpreted in the light of experience.*

We use our ability to shift perception to distinguish our outer experiences from our internal ones, to distinguish objects from people, and ourselves from another. Our sensory capacities—sight, taste, touch, smell, and hearing—orient us toward our relationship with our environment. These five senses ground us in our outer world and determine our relationship to it. The degree of contact we have with our environment—our awareness through all our senses of what is present in the now, not what we imagine being present—determines how rational we are. Ideally, we want to experience congruency, a balance between our inner world and our outer world—our five senses in contact with our environment helps us do that.

Our ability to shift perception begins in the first year of life. Crawling develops the eye muscles needed for shifting perception. After a certain point of maturation, if unable to make perception shifts, children will confuse reality and fantasy when relating events. We accept this confusion of fantasy and reality with very young children and will occasionally tolerate it in children under the age of nine or ten, at which time abstract thinking becomes the norm. Discernment between reality and fantasy is part of the maturation process.

Objective: When focusing on a specific object, students can experience the power of will as an element of concentration and choice.

Materials Needed:

1. Display of weekly quote and title
2. Copies of foreground/background images for each participant (see appendix)
3. A large lightweight colored straight object such as a yardstick or broom handle (instructor stands in front of class with object)
4. Imagery script and calm instrumental background music or weekly recording: Grand Ideas from Within Counselor Edition: Audio-Guided Imagery, Volume 1, track 4, "Points of View" (2:44)
5. Display lesson quote and title

Present Lesson Overview:

Introduce the idea of perception shifts and the acceptance of each person's process for learning with the following expanded activity.

Note: Participants having difficulty with these exercises may have other signs of learning or language processing difficulties.

Directions for activity:

"Look at figure one, focusing on the *white* space first. What does it look like—two faces or a table or a dish?" Pause.

Figure 1

"Shift your perception, your eyes, and focus on the *black*. Now can you see the chalice or table? This is a simple example of shifting perception. Try figure two. Do you see a young girl or an old woman?"

Figure 2

"There is no right or wrong. It is simply white space shared with black—or is it? *It is whatever we choose it to be*—black ink on white paper, maybe. We can live expansively, choosing from the world's limitless possibilities, or we can slowly die with rigidity."

Read imagery script or listen to audio Grand Ideas from Within Counselor Edition, Volume 1, track 4, "Points of View."

Note: For a weekly class of older participants, combine all five days into one session. Do not judge anyone's experience; just acknowledge that everyone has their own unique experience.

Remember to read very slowly, allowing a silent beat at commas, and pause to the count of five at each elliptic.

Day 1: Participants are seated with eyes open and relaxing music playing in the background. Instructor stands in front of group, holding an object in a vertical position extended away from the body.

Imagery Script:

Foreground/Background

1. Say, "Do not speak until directed. Pay attention to your breathing, breathing in and out through your nose. Relaxing your body and looking straight ahead, begin to focus your eyes on the object I am holding. As you continue to breathe, keeping your eyes on the object I am holding, notice what else you can see in the background with your peripheral vision. Now relax your eyes." Pause. "This time, as you breathe in and out, allow your eyes to focus on the environment beyond the object I am holding. Even though you are looking past the object I am holding, at something farther away … because you are choosing to focus on it, it becomes foreground in your mind. Now relax your eyes." Pause.

2. "Once again, breathing in and out, focus on the object I am holding." Pause. "Now shift your eyes to focus beyond the object I am holding." Pause. "Return your gaze back to the object I am holding. Remember, whatever you choose to focus your attention on becomes foreground; everything else is background. Your attention determines what is foreground."

3. "Once again, breathing in and out … direct your attention toward the outside surface of your body, the air on your face, the pressure of your body against the seat … and toward my voice. You may speak to the class. What was that experiment like for you?"

Note: Participants having difficulty with this exercise may have other signs of a learning problem or language processing difficulty.

Day 2: Participants remain seated, eyes open, with relaxing music playing in the background and instructor standing in front of group. The instructor is the object.

Imagery Script:

Peripheral Perception

1. Say, "Do not speak until directed. As you breathe in and out through your nose, relaxing your body and looking straight ahead … you begin to focus your eyes on me. Notice as you continue to breathe, keeping your eyes on me, what else you can see in the background with your peripheral vision."

2. "Now relax your eyes. This time as you breathe in and out, allow your eyes to focus on the environment beyond me. Even though you are looking past me, at something farther away … because you are choosing to focus on something else, it becomes foreground in your mind."

3. "Now relax your eyes." Pause. "Once again, breathing in and out, focus on me. Now shift your eyes to focus beyond me, returning your gaze back to me. Remember, whatever you choose to focus your eyes on becomes foreground; everything else is background. You may speak to the group. How was this time different from yesterday's imagery?"

Note: Notice which participants have difficulty replacing an object of focus with a person; this may be one indication of an anxiety condition from trauma.

Day 3: Participants remain seated with relaxing music playing in the background and eyes closed.

Imagery Script:

Hearing Sensitivity

1. Say, "Do not speak until directed. As you breathe in and out through your nose, closing your eyes, allow my voice to guide you … as all other sounds fall into the background. Becoming more relaxed, move your attention from the outside surface of your body, the air on your face, your relaxing muscles." Pause. "Feeling more relaxed with every thought … you can increase the sensitivity of your hearing." Pause. "Notice the sound of your own breath … the sound of my voice. Find another sound in the room." Pause. "And another outside this room." Pause.

2. "Now allow your ears to choose what to listen to and notice where ears want to go when free to listen to whatever gets their attention." Long pause. "Allowing my voice

to be your foreground sound, continue to breathe in and out through your nose, relaxing your body." Pause. "Remembering whatever you choose to focus your ears or eyes on becomes foreground; everything else is background. Now open your eyes. Softly and slowly, begin to focus your eyes on me, making me your visual foreground. You now have new and useful information about yourself. Relax your eyes." Pause.

3.   "Was shifting your *hearing* harder or easier than shifting your *seeing*? You may speak to the group." Wait for participant response.

Note: Participants having difficulty with this exercise will also have difficulty concentrating when several small group activities are taking place in the room at the same time.

Day 4: This lesson focuses on body sensations and becoming more comfortable with eyes closed. Participants remain seated with relaxing music playing in the background.

Imagery Script:

Body Sensations
Volume 1, track 1, "Points of View"

1.   Say, "Do not speak until directed. As you breathe in and out through your nose, closing your eyes, allow all sounds to fall into the background." Pause. "As you continue to breathe with eyes closed, begin to move your attention to the outside surface of your body." Pause.

2.   "Notice the sensation of air on your face … and now the temperature of the air. Using your mind, shift your attention from the air on your face to your skin touching your clothes." Pause. "Shift to the air between your clothes and skin." Pause. "Sense the temperature of this air." Pause. "Compare this air temperature to the air temperature on your face; notice the difference." Pause.

3.   "As you breathe comfortably, begin to notice or sense the size of the room." Pause. "And relax your attention." Pause.

4.   "Once again, breathing in and out, keeping eyes closed, direct your attention toward my voice … and open your eyes, being present. Remember, whatever you choose to focus your mind on becomes foreground; everything else is background." Pause. "You may speak to the group. What did you learn about yourself?" If a participant replies, "Nothing," simply respond with, "Maybe next time."

Day 5: Focus is on sensing the presence of others. Participants remain seated; begin with relaxing music playing in the background.

Imagery Script:

Sensing Me from You

1. Say, "Do not speak until directed. As you breathe in and out through your nose, relaxing your body, closing your eyes, and using your mind, focus your hearing on the sound of my voice." Pause. "Only one sound … as you continue to breathe with eyes closed, allowing all other sounds to fall into the background … becoming more relaxed with each thought that you have … as you continue to breathe with eyes closed." Pause.

2. "Now, using your mind, locate the person in the room nearest to where you are sitting. Simply sense the air between you and that person." Pause.

3. "Now, again using your mind, locate a different person in the room near to where you are sitting. Simply sense the air between you and that person." Pause.

4. "Now return your mind to the pressure of your body against the seat." Pause. "Remember, whatever you choose to focus your mind on becomes foreground; everything else is background."

5. "Once again, breathing in and out, direct your attention toward my voice and open your eyes, being fully present. You may speak to the group. What did you learn about yourself?"

Note: If participant replies, "Nothing," simply respond with, "Maybe next time."

Verification of Participants' Understanding: (1) Notice participants' verbal response when asked to describe the difference between foreground and background. (2) Ask participants which is easier, shifting their hearing or shifting their seeing? (3) Have participants write in their journals about their experiences or verbally describe their experiences.

Reinforce with Independent Activity: Use the terminology *foreground and background* when introducing a new concept or rule. Refer to the new idea as foreground of the lesson, the idea that rises from the background information. Ask participants, "What background information is needed to apply this new idea in foreground today?" Connect the terms *immaterial information* to the word *background*.

Other Resources:
Seckel, Al. 2003. *The Great Book of Optical Illusion.* Buffalo: Firefly Books.

Additional Notes:

SEEING AND IMAGINING

The eyes are not responsible when the mind does the seeing.

—Publilius Syrus

The real voyage of discovery consists, not in seeking new landscapes, but in having new eyes.

—Marcel Proust

Lesson 4: Distinguish Seeing from Imagining

Grade Level: 4–12

Note: Lessons 4–5 may be done as one session where time permits.

Purpose and Overview: All of our experiences come through our five senses—sight, sound, smell, taste, or touch. Most of us rely on one or two dominant senses that are more highly developed. When we pay attention to the role our senses play in learning, we can use them to bring memories to the surface. The more highly developed each sense is, the better we learn and the better we imagine. Developing our sense of sight, hearing, and touch is an important stepping-stone to *imaging* and *imagining* success in all parts of the participant's life.

You may notice the interchangeable use of *imagery* and *visualization*. This can be confusing because it implies that we are limiting our imagery to visual imagination. Only about 55 percent of the population is visually dominant. The other 45 percent may think that they are unable to use imagery because they do not see things in their imaginations. It is unlikely that any of the participants, even the visual ones, will see with their eyes closed exactly as they see with their eyes open. Reassure participants that their natural way to *imagine* is appropriate in these exercises. There is no right or wrong way to do it. With practice, they will get better at using their imaginations consciously and purposefully.

It is important also to emphasize to participants the difference between *seeing* and *imagining*. At the beginning of the week, the participants actually see with their eyes in order to develop the powers of observation. At the end of the week, the participants close their eyes and see with their mind's eye. For instance, if you ask participants to close their eyes and imagine a friend's face, they will *see* an expression on the friend's face and may *imagine*, based on the expression, what the friend is feeling. If we see someone frown, we may *imagine* the friend is angry, when in reality the friend may be sad, confused, or disappointed. Therefore, each participant's imagining will be unique and creative, but all observers can see what is seen—concrete and verifiable.

Objective: Participants will be able to distinguish the difference between *seeing* and *imagining,* a basic tenant of mental health.

Materials Needed:
1. Imagery script or, for weekly session, Grand Ideas from Within Counselor Edition: Audio-Guided Imagery, Volume 1, track 5, "Seeing and Imagining" (5:18)
2. Display lesson quote and title
3. Verify participants' ability to shift perception through included imagery.

Present Lesson Overview:
Read Imagery Script:
Day 1: Participants remain seated, relaxing music playing in the background and materials at hand.

Imagery Script:
Seeing versus Imagining
1. Say, "Do not speak until directed. Put your head down on your arms on the edge of your desk or table so you are able to see your lap." Pause until participants are settled. "As you breathe in and out through your nose … allow my voice to guide you … as all … other … sounds fall into the background."
2. "Breathing in and out through your nose, look at the rise and fall of your chest as you breathe slowly and easily." Pause for fifteen seconds. "Notice the soft, gentle movement of your body as you breathe…perhaps your stomach also rises with the in breath. Perhaps, you can see a subtle movement of your legs on the chair with each inhale and exhale."
3. "Without judging … simply observing … look at your shirt. Notice its details … the way the fabric moves … the patterns created as you breathe … the colors of your

shirt … any stitching, buttons, or decorations it may have." Pause. "Look again at the rise and fall of your chest."

4. "Then move your attention to the air on your face and the pressure of your body against the seat and your feet on the floor, feeling relaxed." Pause. "Sitting up straight, being fully present and ready to work." Pause.

5. "You have one minute to write about or draw your experience. When you are finished, put your pencil down and sit quietly." Pause one minute. "You may speak to the group."

Day 2: Participants remain seated, relaxing music playing in the background and materials at hand.

1. Say, "Do not speak until directed. Put your head down on your arms on the edge of your desk or table so you are able to see your lap." Pause until participants are settled. "As you breathe in and out through your nose … allow my voice to guide you … as all … other … sounds fall into the background."

1. "As you breathe … in and out through your nose and look at the rise and fall of your chest, continue breathing slowly and easily." Pause. "Watch the movement of your body as you breathe … Perhaps your stomach rises with the in breath … Perhaps with each inhale and exhale, you can see a subtle movement of your legs on the chair. Allow your eyes to gather information."

2. "Without judging, simply observing, look at your belt, pants, or skirt. Notice the details … the way the material moves … the patterns created as you breathe … the color … any stitching, buttons, or decorations it may have." Pause.

3. "Look again at the rise and fall of your chest. Then move your attention to the outside surface of your body … the air on your face and the pressure of your body against the seat and your feet on the floor, sitting up straight, feeling relaxed … being fully present and ready to work." Pause.

4. "You will have one minute to write about or draw something you saw in your mind's eye. When you are finished, put your pencil down and sit quietly." Pause one minute. "You may speak to the group."

Day 3: Participants remain seated, relaxing music playing in the background and materials at hand.

Imagery Script:

Creative Imagining

1. Say, "Do not speak until directed. Put your head down on your desk if you wish." Pause until participants are settled. "As you breathe in and out through your nose... closing your eyes, allow my voice to guide you... as all... other... sounds fall into the background. Becoming more relaxed, move your attention from the outside surface of your body and the air on your face to your relaxing muscles." Pause. "Feeling more relaxed with every thought ... allow yourself to journey inward." Pause.

2. "As you breathe in and out through your nose, begin to see in your mind's eye an ordinary window." Pause. "Notice the size, the shape, and the way the light reflects off the surface." Pause.

3. "Now you are going to redesign the window. Use your mind to shape it into any shape you wish. Perhaps you'll add more panes ... or take away the panes altogether. Perhaps you'll make an arched frame ... or add colors or pictures to the panes. Watch it take on its new form—one of your design." Pause. "Get a clear picture of your window in your mind's eye." Pause.

4. "Now move your attention away from the window to the outside surface of your body ... the air on your face and the pressure of your body against the seat and your feet on the floor, sitting up straight and feeling relaxed, opening your eyes, being fully present and ready to work." Pause.

5. "You have one minute to draw the window you designed. When you are finished, put your pencil down and sit quietly. One minute pause. "You may speak to the group."

Day 4: Participants remain seated, relaxing music playing in the background and materials at hand.

1. Say, "Do not speak until directed. As you breathe in and out through your nose... closing your eyes, allow my voice to guide you ... as all ... other ... sounds fall into the background. Becoming more relaxed, move your attention from the outside surface of your body ... and the air on your face... to your relaxing muscles, feeling more relaxed with every thought. Pause. "Allow yourself to journey inward." Pause.

2. "As you breathe in and out through your nose, begin to see in your mind's eye the window you previously designed." Pause. "Notice the size and the way the light reflects off of it." Pause.

3. "Now add a holiday decoration to the window. Choose whatever holiday you wish and add a decoration to your window. You might want to paint or stencil a design or

pattern on the glass, or perhaps you would like to add something to the outside, or maybe you would just like to change the glass from clear to a color." Pause fifteen seconds.

4. "Get a clear picture in your mind's eye of the holiday window decoration you have designed." Pause. "Now move your attention away from the window to the outside surface of your body … the air on your face … the pressure of your body against the seat and your feet on the floor … sitting up straight and feeling relaxed … opening your eyes … being fully present and ready to work." Pause.

5. "You have one minute to draw your window and holiday decoration. When you are finished, put your pencil down and sit quietly." One minute pause. "You may speak to the group."

Day 5: Participants remain seated, relaxing music playing in the background and materials at hand.

1. Say, "Do not speak until directed. As you breathe in and out through your nose [pause], closing your eyes, allow my voice to guide you … as all … other…sounds fall into the background. Becoming more relaxed, move your attention from the outside surface of your body… and the air on your face … to your relaxing muscles." Pause. "Feeling more relaxed with every thought … allow yourself to journey inward." Pause.

2. "As you breathe in and out through your nose, begin to see in your mind's eye the window you previously designed. Notice the size and the way the light reflects off of it." Pause.

3. "Now you are going to design curtains or a covering for your window. Your covering may be plain or fancy … colorful or neutral … textured or smooth … patterned or not." Pause. "The curtains may be closed or open. Just allow your imagination to create the perfect covering for your window." Pause fifteen seconds.

4. "Get a clear picture of your newly decorated window in your mind's eye." Pause. "When you are finished, move your attention away from the window to the outside surface of your body, the air on your face, and the pressure of your body against the seat and your feet on the floor, feeling relaxed … opening your eyes, being fully present and ready to work." Pause.

5. You have one minute to draw the window and curtains you designed. When you are finished, put your pencil down and sit quietly." Pause one minute. "You may speak to the group."

Verification of Participants' Understanding: Participant is able to demonstrate knowing the difference between seeing characteristics of expression and their imagined meaning of the expression.

Reinforce with Independent Activity: Ask participants to begin to notice more detail in what they see all around them. Encourage them to imagine how they might change everyday objects to suit their fancy—the beginning of creativity and individuality.

Other Resource:

Bourne, Edmund J. 2000. *The Anxiety and Phobia Workbook, Third Edition.* Oakland: New Harbinger Publications.

Additional Notes:

HEARING WHAT I HEAR

None of us will ever accomplish anything excellent or commanding
except when he listens to this whisper, which is heard by him alone.

—Ralph Waldo Emerson

Lesson 5: Imagery with the Sense of Hearing

Grade Level: 4–12

Purpose and Overview: When we realize the role our sense of hearing plays in learning, we can use it to bring memories to the surface. Most of us use music to create or re-create a mood and can remember where we first heard our favorite song or may even be able to notice that a song popping into our minds may clue us in as to how we are feeling in the moment.

Don Campbell, author of *The Mozart Effect,* raised our awareness of the important role music can play in the learning process. According to his research, sound changes brain waves, and music in certain tempos can enhance learning. Campbell, in *Rhythms of Learning: Creative Tools for Developing Lifelong Learning*, coauthored with Chris Brewer, states, "A guided imagery session can be an important technique for learning new material or reviewing information. The use of music and the relaxed presentation anchors the information in the memory system effectively."

The intent of the following imagery is to raise the participants' awareness of personal auditory capabilities, recognizing external sounds before seeking internal sounds. Any teaching exercise (math, history, science, social studies, and so) can use sounds and music to anchor learning.

Objective: Participant will be able to discern external sounds and create mentally imagined sounds.

Materials Needed:
1. Imagery script, relaxing music, or recording of Grand Ideas from Within: Audio-Guided Imagery, Volume 1, track 6, "Sounds of Nature" (5:33)

2. Display of lesson quote and title

Present Lesson Overview:
Engage participants in calming themselves, listening, and discerning sounds in the immediate and then extended environment.

Read Imagery Script:
Note: If presenting only once weekly, with younger participants, combine days 1 and 2. For older participants, combine days 1, 4, and 5 or play Volume 1, track 6, "Sounds of Nature."

Imagery Script:

Hearing What I Hear

Day 1: (Actual sounds) Participants remain seated with relaxing music playing in the background.

1. Say, "Do not speak until directed. As you breathe in and out through your nose, closing your eyes, allow my voice to guide you… as all … other … sounds fall into the background. Becoming more relaxed… move your attention from the outside surface of your body… and the air on your face … to your relaxing muscles." Pause. "Feeling more relaxed with every thought … allow yourself to journey inward." Pause, fading out music so only your voice is heard.

2. "As you breathe in and out through your nose, begin to notice the sounds you can actually hear in the room. In addition to my voice, perhaps you notice the sound of a fan … or someone shifting in their chair. Listen for sounds outside the room … or to your own breath. For one minute, which is all the time you need, use your mind to guide your ears from one sound to another, finding as many sounds as you can identify in the next minute." Pause one minute.

3. "Now move your attention away from the sounds around you to the outside surface of your body … the air on your face, the pressure of your body against the seat, and your feet on the floor, feeling relaxed … opening your eyes, being fully present and ready to work." Pause.

4. "You have one minute to write about all the sounds you heard with your ears. When you are finished, put your pencil down and sit quietly." Pause one minute and fade in music. "You may speak to the group."

Day 2: (Imagined sounds of nature) Participants remain seated with relaxing music playing in the background.

1. Say, "Do not speak until directed. As you breathe in and out through your nose … closing your eyes, allow my voice to guide you … as all … other … sounds fall into the background. Becoming more relaxed … move your attention from the outside surface of your body … and the air on your face … to your relaxing muscles … feeling more relaxed with every thought … allow yourself to journey inward." Pause and fade out music.

2. "As you breathe in and out through your nose, begin to listen in your memory or *hear in your mind* the following sounds." Pause between phrases so the participant has time to create imagined sounds. "A bird singing … the wind in the trees … a waterfall … thunder, a soft gentle rain … a hailstorm … frogs croaking … waves lapping on the shore … leaves falling from the trees … a bee … a mosquito … a dog … a cat … a tree limb falling to the ground." Pause. "All these sounds are imagined. Now, for thirty seconds, which is all the time you need, imagine any other nature sounds." Wait thirty seconds.

3. "Now moving your attention away from the sounds of nature to the outside surface of your body … the air on your face, the pressure of your body against the seat, and your feet on the floor, feeling relaxed … open your eyes, being fully present and ready to work." Pause.

4. "You have one minute to write about all the sounds you can recall hearing in your imagination. When you finish, put your pencil down and sit quietly." Pause one minute and fade in music. "You may speak to the group."

Day 3: (Imagined sounds) Participants remain seated with relaxing music playing in the background.

1. Say, "Do not speak until directed. As you breathe in and out through your nose … closing your eyes, allow my voice to guide you … as all … other … sounds fall into the background. Becoming more relaxed … moving your attention from the outside surface of your body … and the air on your face … to your relaxing muscles; feeling more relaxed with every thought, and allowing yourself to journey inward." Pause.

2. "As you breathe in and out through your nose, begin to imagine or hear in your mind the following sounds." Pause briefly between phrases: "An automobile starting … an automobile running … an automobile horn … an automobile stopping … an

automobile stuck in the mud … a diesel truck running … a diesel truck horn … a motorcycle running … a bus running … a train moving down the track … a train whistle … a boat moving through the water … a boat horn … a bicycle in motion … a bicycle bell … a skateboard jumping a curb … Rollerblades on the street." Pause. "Now, for thirty seconds, which is all the time you need, imagine any other sounds of things in motion or machines running."

3. "Now move your attention away from the sounds in your mind to the outside surface of your body to the air on your face, the pressure of your body against the seat and your feet on the floor, feeling relaxed." Pause. "Open your eyes, being fully present and ready to work."

4. "You have one minute to write about all the sounds you heard in your head. When you are finished, put your pencil down and sit quietly." Pause one minute. "You may speak to the group."

Day 4: Participants remain seated with relaxing music playing in the background.

1. Say, "Do not speak until directed. As you breathe in and out through your nose … closing your eyes, allowing my voice to guide you. Using your ears, hearing [supply sounds that can be heard by everyone in the room] _____, _____, and _____."

2. "Becoming more relaxed, move your attention from the outside of your body … and the air on your face … to your relaxing muscles." Pause. "Feeling more relaxed with every thought, allow yourself to journey inward." Pause.

3. "As you breathe in and out through your nose, begin to imagine or hear in your mind the following sounds: radio playing … the table being set for dinner … dishes being put away … people talking and laughing … the television playing … the phone ringing … someone typing on a computer … popcorn popping; the microwave bell … a baby crying … siblings fighting … a book's pages turning … writing in longhand … bathwater running." Pause.

4. "For thirty seconds, which is all the time you need, imagine any other sounds you might hear at your home."

5. "Now move your attention away from the sounds of home to the outside surface of your body … the air on your face, the pressure of your body against the seat and your feet on the floor, to the sounds in the room, feeling relaxed … opening your eyes, being fully present and ready to work." Pause.

6. "You have one minute to write in your journal the sounds you remember from this session. When you are finished, put your pencil down and sit quietly." One minute pause. "You may speak to the group."

Day 5: (Imagined sounds) Participants remain seated with relaxing music playing in the background.

1. Say, "Do not speak until directed. As you breathe in and out through your nose, close your eyes and allow my voice to guide you ... as all ... other ... sounds fall into the background. Becoming more relaxed, move your attention from the outside surface of your body and the air on your face ... to your relaxing muscles." Pause. "Feeling more relaxed with every thought ... allow yourself to journey inward." Pause.

2. "As you breathe in and out through your nose, begin to imagine or *hear in your mind* the following sounds: a drum ... a harp ... a tuba ... a violin ... a trumpet ... a clarinet ... a flute ... a bass fiddle ... a guitar ... a tambourine ... a cymbal ... a bell ... a bass drum." Pause. "Now, for thirty seconds, which is all the time you need, imagine the sound of a band—perhaps a marching band, or a rock band, or a country band, or a jazz band, a school band, or a symphony. Just fill your mind with the sound of music of your choice." Pause for thirty seconds.

3. Now move your attention away from the music in your mind, to the music playing in this room, to the outside surface of your body ... the air on your face, the pressure of your body against the seat and your feet on the floor. Feeling relaxed ... opening your eyes, being fully present and ready to work." Pause.

4. "You have one minute to write in your journal all the sounds you heard in your imagination. When you are finished, put your pencil down and sit quietly." Pause one minute. "You may speak to the group."

Verification of Participants' Understanding: Briefly allow participants to talk about what they noticed this week as a result of this week's exercises. You might ask them to describe the type of band or musical group they heard. Do not judge anyone's experience; acknowledge that everyone has his or her own unique and valuable experience.

Reinforce with Independent Activity: Ask participants to begin to notice the sounds that get their attention throughout the day. Encourage them to experiment with music to enhance certain activities—studying, relaxing, eating, and sleeping. Have participants notice whether any particular sound or types of sounds enhance or distract from the activity at hand.

Other Resources:

Brewer, Chris, and Campbell, Don G. 1991. *Rhythms of Learning: Creative Tools for Developing Lifelong Learning.* Tucson: Cephyr Press.

Murdock, Maureen. 1987. *Spinning Inward: Using Guided Imagery with Children for Learning, Creativity & Relaxation.* Boston: Shambhala Publications.

Van Kuiken D. 2004 "A Meta-analysis of the Effect of Guided Imagery Practice on Outcomes". *Journal of Holistic Nursing.* 22, 2: 164–179.

Kabat-Zinn, Jon, PhD.1990. *Full Catastrophe Living: Using the Wisdom of Your Body and Mind to Face Stress, Pain, and Illness.* New York: Bantam Doubleday Dell Publishing Group.

Additional Notes:

SENSING THE WORLD AROUND ME

The senses collect the surface facts of matter … It was sensation; when memory came, it was experience; when mind acted, it was knowledge; when mind acted on it as knowledge, it was thought.

—Ralph Waldo Emerson

For the sense of smell, almost more than any other, has the power to recall memories and it's a pity that you use it so little.

—Rachel Carson

Lesson 6: Physical Sensations, Kinesthesia

Grade Level: 4–12

Purpose and Overview: As a culture, we are preoccupied with body image—how we look. Yet simultaneously, most of us are completely out of touch with sensing our bodies. Not many of us use our gift of sensing as a means of gaining deeper insight into the reality of our experience. Jon Kabat-Zinn, in his book *Full Catastrophe Living,* discusses at length the relationship between body sensations, emotions, and physical and emotional health. When we fail to become comfortable with our bodies as they are, we create problems with touching and being touched and therefore with intimacy. According to Kabat-Zinn, "Our *thoughts about our body* can limit drastically the range of feelings we allow ourselves to experience." However, he goes on to say, "When we put energy into actually *experiencing our bodies* and we refuse to get caught up in the overlay of *judgmental thinking about it,* our whole view of it and of ourselves can change dramatically."

Kinesthesia is the physical sense our bodies produce when we physically experience temperature, pressure, weight, pain, and tension. We often move to change our position in order to become more comfortable or to alleviate discomfort without giving our movement any thought. We just do it. For instance, we may choose to deal with muscle tension by taking medicine to relieve the tension—simply making the discomfort *go away.* A healthier choice would be to recognize the source of tension as muscle tightness and relieve it by a few simple stretching exercises—a simple process of acknowledging and taking responsibility for body sensations.

We often confuse body sensations (Kinesthesia) with emotions. Emotions communicate our *internal* feelings: *gladness, anger, sadness, and fear.* When we feel the emotions called *anger* and *fear*, we may want to move in rage toward the source or in fear away from the source to avoid inflicting or encountering kinesthetic external pain. Some people turn their anger inward which is a bad idea. Anger is meant to be directed outward. Similarly, some turn fear inward and freeze while others move toward their fear object or situation in order to get their fearful feelings over.

When we feel the emotion of sadness, we try to distract ourselves to avoid the *internal* physical discomfort usually felt in the chest area, to avoid crying. When we experience gladness, we tend to want to move with excitement, to share it.

Sensations and emotions do not come from the object or person we perceive but from our body's response to our external and internal environments dancing with our mental attitude. This is why people have different sensations, emotions, or opinions about the same person/object.

When we take the time to become the *observer* of our sensations and emotions, then we are more likely to act in healthy ways. Learning to *observe* and *discern* our own body sensations and thoughts—physical, emotional, and mental—helps us realize that our emotions are of our own creation and we are the ones responsible for them. We can use our minds and *decide,* depending upon our interpretation of the external stimulus, to be comfortable or uncomfortable—and to act on our own behalf.

Because all sensations are important to our experience of reality, it is also important to bring the participants' attention to the value of taste and smell in the enrichment of our lives and our everyday experiences. It is a fact that an experience that arouses all of our senses is more memorable than one in which we have minimal sensory involvement. To achieve physical and emotional well-being, we must be aware of the different boundaries between our physical surroundings as perceived by our five senses, our body sensations, and our mental thoughts.

Objective: Participants will be able to develop an awareness of *body sensations*—touch, motion, temperature, taste, and smell—important components of physical and emotional well-being. (Future lessons focus on emotions.)

Materials Needed:
1. Imagery script or Grand Ideas from Within audio, Volume 1, track 7, "Sensing"
2. Display of lesson quote and title

Present Lesson Overview:

Point out that at any given moment, there is an odor and a taste, even when there are no words to name or describe it.

Read imagery script or listen to Grand Ideas from Within audio, Volume 1, track 7, "Sensing" (5:33).

Imagery Script:

Seeing Inside

Day 1: Participants remain seated with relaxing music playing in the background.

1. Say, "Do not speak until directed. As you breathe in and out through your nose, closing your eyes ... allow my voice to guide you ... as all ... other ... sounds fall into the background. Becoming more relaxed, move your attention from the outside surface of your body ... and the air on your face ... to your relaxing muscles." Pause. "Feeling more relaxed with every thought, allow yourself to journey inward." Pause.

2. "Bringing your attention to your skin ... noticing how it feels ... whether it is chapped and dry or moist and soft. Perhaps your face is flush, warm ... Maybe the air in the room feels cool on your skin or maybe there is a gentle flow of air in the room lightly touching your skin." Pause.

3. "Perhaps you are aware of your clothing touching your skin, where it feels scratchy ... stiff ... tight ... or itchy ... where it feels soft ... loose ... and comfortable." Pause. Noticing the feel of the other things touching your skin ... perhaps how a lock of hair feels as it touches your face or neck ... or the feel of any jewelry you may be wearing— the weight or pressure of it." Pause.

4. "Notice the feel of the surface your fingers are resting upon—smooth or rough ... warm or cool ... soft or hard." Pause. "Feeling your shoes on your feet ... where they touch ... whether there is discomfort or comfort." Pause.

5. "Then very slowly wiggle your feet, hands, arms, and legs ... moving your attention to the outside surface of your body ... to the air on your face and the pressure of your body against the seat, feeling relaxed and alert ... opening your eye ... being fully present and ready to work." Pause.

6. Now breathing easily and naturally, take a moment to write about or draw what sensations you noticed in this exercise that previously went unnoticed. When you are finished, put your pencil down and sit quietly." Pause one minute. "You may speak to the group."

Day 2: Participants remain seated with relaxing music playing in the background.

1. Say, "Do not speak until directed. As you breathe in and out through your nose … closing your eyes, allow my voice to guide you … as all … other … sounds fall into the background. Becoming more relaxed … move your attention from the outside surface of your body and the air on your face … to your relaxing muscles." Pause. "Feeling more relaxed with every thought … allow yourself to journey inward." Pause.

2. "Begin to notice the places on your body where you feel pressure, starting at the top of your head…pressure from a hat or hair ornaments. What about your neck, shoulders, or arms …? Any pressure on your chest or back where you are touching the desk or where your clothing may be too tight? Feel how the pressure changes as you breathe in and out." Pause.

3. "Feel where your arms and hands are resting and feel if there is any pressure there. Is there pressure on your waist and hips? Any binding from your clothing or pressure where your body touches the chair?" Pause. "What about your legs? … Feel where they touch the chair … and perhaps where you have them crossed at the knee or ankle … or where your clothing touches your knee … feel your ankles and feet. What is touching them … your socks … your shoes … the floor?" Pause.

4. "Then very slowly wiggle your feet, hands, arms, and legs … moving your attention to the outside surface of your body … to the air on your face and the pressure of your body against the seat, feeling relaxed and alert … Open your eyes, being fully present and ready to work." Pause.

5. "Now, breathing easily and naturally, take a minute to write about or draw the body sensations you noticed in this exercise that previously went unnoticed. When you are finished, put your pencil down and sit quietly. Pause one minute. "You may speak to the group."

Day 3: Participants remain seated with relaxing music playing in the background.

1. Say, "Do not speak until directed. As you breathe in and out through your nose … closing your eyes, allow my voice to guide you … as all … other … sounds fall into

the background. Becoming more relaxed ... move your attention from the outside surface of your body ... and the air on your face ... to your relaxing muscles." Pause. "Feeling more relaxed with every thought ... allow yourself to journey inward." Pause.

2. "With your eyes closed, you cannot *see* the people in the room, but you may be able to *feel* their presence. They may be sitting close by. Are you able to feel the space or distance between you and others? Put your *feelers* out and sense if you can *feel* the location of the person you like the best in the room." Pause.

3. "Notice how easy it may be for your energy to travel to just one person." Pause. Now try to *feel* the location of the person in the room that you like the least. Notice if it is more or less difficult for your energy to move in that direction." Pause.

4. "Take one minute, which is all the time you need, to send your feelers out to touch each of the individuals in the room." Pause for one minute.

5. "Bring your *feelers* back to your space ... feeling the rise and fall of your breath ... feeling your body in the chair ... and your feet on the floor. Very slowly, wiggle your feet, hands, arms, and legs. Move your attention to the outside surface of your body to the air on your face and the pressure of your body against the seat, feeling relaxed and alert ... Open your eyes, being fully present and ready to work." Pause.

6. "Now, breathing easily and naturally, take a minute to write or draw about your experience. When you are finished, put your pencil down and sit quietly." Pause one minute. "You may speak to the group."

Day 4: Participants remain seated with relaxing music playing in the background.

1. Say, "Do not speak until directed. As you breathe in and out through your nose ... closing your eyes, allow my voice to guide you ... as all ... other ... sounds fall into the background. Becoming more relaxed ... moving your attention from the outside surface of your body ... and the air on your face ... to your relaxing muscles ... feeling more relaxed with every thought ... allowing yourself to journey inward." Pause.

2. With your eyes closed, you cannot *see* the objects in the room but you may be able to *feel* their presence. Notice the difference in these feelings. Send your *feelers* out to other objects in the room, such as your chair ... the _____, or _____, or other objects." Pause for one minute. "Now feel the presence of someone close by ... shift back and forth between your feeling of objects and your feeling of people." Long pause.

3. "Gently bring your *feelers* back to your space ... feeling the rise and fall of your breath ... wiggling your feet, hands, arms, and legs. Pause. Moving your attention to the outside surface of your body [pause], to the air on your face and the pressure of

your body against the seat, feeling relaxed and alert ... open your eyes ... being fully present ... and ready to work." Pause.

4. "Now, breathing easily and naturally, take out your pencil and journal. Take a moment to write about the difference between feeling a person's presence and feeling the presence of an object. When you are finished, put your pencil down and sit quietly." Pause one minute. "You may speak to the group."

Day 5: Participants remain seated with relaxing music playing in the background.

1. Say, "Do not speak until I direct you to do so ... closing your eyes as all ... other ... sounds fall into the background. You can journey inward and allow my voice to guide you as you begin to feel relaxation flow into your body as if it were being poured through an opening in your head ... moving through your neck, arms, torso, legs, and feet, filling your body with warmth, relaxation, and perhaps color." Pause.

2. "With your eyes closed, you cannot *see* the boundaries of the room ... but you may be able to *feel* their presence. Once again, using your mind, send your *feelers* out to locate the walls of the room ... noticing which is closest ... which is farthest away ... Feel where the windows and doors are located ... which walls have objects on or in front of them ... just exploring the boundaries of the room and whether or not the walls feel different to you." Pause. "And now, bringing your attention to the ceiling and floor ... exploring them with your *feelers*. How do they feel ... different or the same?" Pause. "Allowing your *feelers* to move out through one of the windows or doors, you can experience what that is like." Pause.

3. "Then gently bring your *feelers* back to your space ... feeling the boundaries of you ... *your* space—the imaginary protective box or cylinder that surrounds and contains you in this moment ... and any other moment you choose." Pause.

4. "Then slowly bring your attention to the rise and fall of your breath ... feeling your body in the chair ... wiggling your feet, hands, arms, and legs. Moving your attention to the outside surface of your body ... to the air on your face and the pressure of your body against the seat, feeling relaxed and alert. Open your eyes, being fully present and ready to work." Pause.

5. "Now, breathing easily and naturally, take a moment to write about or draw your experience. When you are finished, put your pencil down and sit quietly." Pause one minute. "You may speak to the group."

Verification of Participants' Understanding: Discussions will indicate participants' ability to distinguish between physical sensations and imagined ones.

Reinforce with Independent Activity: Encourage participants to notice their body sensations, where their *feelers* are at different times of the day during different experiences or activities. Suggest they pay attention to their senses when they are playing with a friend, taking a test, eating a meal, disagreeing with a parent, listening to the radio, or looking at a book. Direct them to observe when their body tenses or stresses and how they can reduce stress by slowing the breath and bringing calming sights, sounds, or smells to mind.

Other Resources:

Bourne, Edmund J. 2000. *The Anxiety and Phobia Workbook, Third Edition*. Oakland: New Harbinger Publications.

Brewer, Chris and Campbell, Don G. 1991. *Rhythms of Learning: Creative Tools for Developing Lifelong Learning*. Tucson: Cephyr Press.

Murdock, Maureen. 1987. *Spinning Inward: Using Guided Imagery with Children for Learning, Creativity & Relaxation*. Boston: Shambhala Publications.

Additional Notes:

SMELLING AND TASTING

For the sense of smell, almost more than any other, has the power
to recall memories and it is a pity that you use it so little.

—Rachel Carson

Lesson 7: Smell and Taste (optional for older participants)

Grade Level: 6–8

Purpose and Overview: It is a fact that an experience that arouses all of our senses is more memorable than one in which we have minimal sensory involvement. Much is written about the importance of incorporating sight, sound, and feeling into a learning experience, but much less is said about taste and smell. Yet who can deny the powerful memory that comes forth when tasting a re-creation of Grandma's apple pie or smelling the scent of a former loved one's fragrance? Who can fail to recognize the importance of taste and smell when a stuffy nose blocks them?

Because all sensations are important to our experience of reality, it is important to bring the participants' attention to the value of taste and smell in the enrichment of our lives and our everyday experience.

Objective: Participants become aware of their creative internal resources through smells and tastes—important components of physical and emotional well-being.

Materials Needed:
1. Display of weekly title and quote
2. Participants' journal and writing or drawing instrument
3. Grand Ideas from Within: Audio-Guided Imagery,
4. lesson 7, day 1,
5. Grand Ideas from Within Counselor Edition, audio track 10, "Relaxing Music" if reading days 1–4 script.

Note: Days 3 and 4 of this lesson are optional

Days 1–5: Participants seated with materials

Imagery Script:

Smelling and Tasting

Day 1: Participants remain seated with relaxing music playing in the background.

1. Say, "Do not speak until directed. As you breathe in and out through your nose … closing your eyes, allow my voice to guide you … as all … other … sounds fall into the background. Becoming more relaxed … move your attention from the outside surface of your body … and the air on your face … to your relaxing muscles." Pause. "Feeling more relaxed with every thought … allow yourself to journey inward." Pause.

2. "Slowly bring your attention to your mouth … and tongue … and the taste that is present in your mouth at this time. Perhaps your mouth has the fresh clean taste of the cool sip of water you had a short time ago … or the toothpaste you used this morning … or the lingering taste of your last meal … or the present taste of gum or candy."

3. "Imagine the smell of your favorite food … and now the taste. Pause one minute.

4. "Now, gently moving your attention to the outside surface of your body … feeling the air on your face and the pressure of your body against the seat, feeling relaxed." Pause. "Open your eyes when you are ready, being fully present and ready to work." Pause.

5. "Now, breathing easily and naturally, take a moment to write about or draw your experience. When you are finished, put your pencil down and sit quietly." Pause one minute. "You may speak to the group."

Day 2: Participants remain seated with relaxing music playing in the background.

1. Say, "Do not speak until directed. As you breathe in and out through your nose … closing your eyes, allow my voice to guide you … as all … other … sounds fall into the background. Becoming more relaxed … move your attention from the outside surface of your body … and the air on your face … to your relaxing muscles [pause]. Feeling more relaxed with every thought … allow yourself to journey inward." Pause.

2. "Slowly bring your attention to your mouth … and tongue and the taste that is present in your mouth at this time … Now to your nose—and the smell that is in the foreground for you." Pause. "Gently expand your awareness to other smells in the

room. Perhaps you notice the smell of your clothing ... or skin ... your books, the fragrance of another person in the room, the smell of the air. Just take a moment to explore the smells around you ... and any tastes that may be associated with those smells." Pause one minute.

3. "Now gently moving your attention to the outside surface of your body [pause], feeling the air on your face and the pressure of your body against the seat, feeling relaxed (pause), opening your eyes as you are ready, being fully present and ready to work." Pause.

4. Now, breathing easily and naturally, take a moment to write about or draw your experience. When you are finished, put your pencil down and sit quietly." Pause for one minute. "You may speak to the group."

Day 3: Participants remain seated with relaxing music playing in the background.

1. Say, "Do not speak until directed. As you breathe in and out through your nose ... closing your eyes, allow my voice to guide you ... as all ... other ... sounds fall into the background. Becoming more relaxed ... move your attention from the outside surface of your body and the air on your face ... to your relaxing muscles." Pause. "Feeling more relaxed with every thought ... allow yourself to journey inward." Pause.

2. "Slowly bring your attention to your mouth ... and tongue ... and the taste that is present in your mouth at this time ... and the smell that might be associated with this taste." Pause.

3. "Now move in your imagination to your favorite eating place or places." Pause. "Perhaps you are in the kitchen at home, or your grandmother's house, or your favorite restaurant, or a friend's home, or a favorite picnic spot, or your church or school. Spend a minute, which is all the time you need, and allow yourself to experience the smells and tastes of your most favorite eating places." Pause one minute.

4. "Now gently moving your attention to the outside surface of your body ... feeling the air on your face and the pressure of your body against the seat, feeling relaxed ... open your eyes when you are ready, being fully present and ready to work." Pause.

5. "Now, breathing easily and naturally, take a minute to write about or draw your experience. When you are finished, put your pencil down and sit quietly." Pause one minute. You may speak to the group."

Day 4: Participants remain seated with relaxing music playing in the background.

1. Say, "Do not speak until directed. As you breathe in and out through your nose ... closing your eyes, allow my voice to guide you ... as all ... other ... sounds fall into the background. Becoming more relaxed ... move your attention from the outside surface of your body ... and the air on your face ... to your relaxing muscles." Pause. "Feeling more relaxed with every thought ... allow yourself to journey inward." Pause.

2. "Slowly bring your attention to your mouth ... and tongue ... and the taste that is present in your mouth at this time ... and any smell that may be associated with that taste." Pause.

3. "Now gently moving your attention to the outside surface of your body [pause], feeling the air on your face and the pressure of your body against the seat, feeling relaxed [pause]; slowly open your eyes, allowing them to rest on an object in the room. Imagine how that objects smells ... and tastes." Pause. "Move your eyes to a different object and imagine how it smells ... and tastes [pause], moving on to a third object." Pause.

4. "Now, breathing easily and naturally, take a minute to write about or draw your experience. When you are finished, put your pencil down and sit quietly." Pause one-minute pause. "You may speak to the group."

Day 5: Participants remain seated with relaxing music playing in the background.

1. Say, "Do not speak until directed. As you breathe in and out through your nose ... closing your eyes ... allow my voice to guide you ... as all ... other ... sounds fall into the background. Becoming more relaxed ... move your attention from the outside surface of your body ... and the air on your face ... to your relaxing muscles." Pause. "Feeling more relaxed with every thought ... allow yourself to journey inward." Pause. "Keep your eyes closed and remember an object in the room. Pause. "Explore it as you see it in your mind, using all of your five senses." Pause. "Notice the details of design or color ... Imagine how it feels when you hold it ... the texture ... the weight ... the shape of it." Pause. "Now taste it and smell it with your mind." Pause. "Hear the sound associated with this object." Pause. "Take a moment to explore fully, using all of your senses, any other item in the room you can remember, keeping your eyes closed." Pause for thirty seconds.

2. "Now gently move your attention to the outside surface of your body … feeling the air on your face and the pressure of your body against the seat, feeling relaxed … being fully present and ready to work." Pause.

3. "Now, breathing easily and naturally, take a minute to write about or draw your experience. When you are finished, put your pencil down and sit quietly." Pause one minute. "You may speak to the group."

Verification of Participants' Understanding: Participants' journal writing will indicate a connection to taste and smell. Ask participants to share any surprises in the exercises relating to taste and smell. Do not judge anyone's experience; focus instead on each person's uniqueness.

Reinforce with Independent Activity: Encourage participants to notice each sense during different experiences or activities. Suggest they pay attention to their senses when they are playing with a friend, taking a test, eating a meal, disagreeing with a parent, listening to the radio, or looking at a book. Direct them to observe when the body tenses or stresses and how they can reduce stress by slowing the breath while bring calming sights, sounds, or smells to mind.

Other Resources:

Bourne, Edmund J. 2000 *The Anxiety and Phobia Workbook, Third Edition,* Oakland: New Harbinger Publications.

Brewer, Chris and Campbell, Don G. 1991. *Rhythms of Learning: Creative Tools for Developing Lifelong Learning.* Tucson: Cephyr Press.

Murdock, Maureen. 1987. *Spinning Inward: Using Guided Imagery with Children for Learning, Creativity & Relaxation.* 300 Boston: Shambhala Publications.

Additional Notes:

LESSONS 8–11
SAFETY NEEDS

SECURITY AND STABILITY

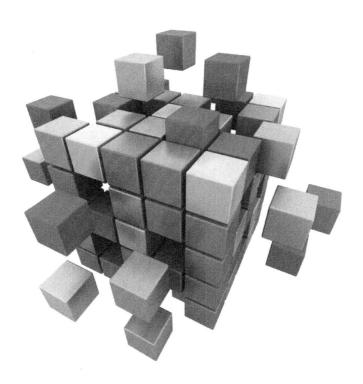

FEELING SAFE

Fear comes from uncertainty. When we are absolutely certain, whether of our worth or worthlessness, we are almost impervious to fear.

—William Congreve

Lesson 8: A Safe Place within Self

Grade Level: 3–12

Purpose and Overview: We all need to feel safe and secure in order to be and do our best. Many of us, however, may not have places in our lives where we feel safe—sometimes because there is no physical safety in our home or family environment and sometimes because there is no *perceived* safety due to anxiety or mood problems.

Abraham Maslow, one of the founders of humanistic psychology, arranged human needs like a ladder. At the bottom are the most basic physical needs: air, water, food, sex. On the next step are safety needs: security, stability. Psychological or social needs—belonging, love, and acceptance—make up the third ladder rung, and at the top of the ladder are the self-actualizing needs: the need to fulfill oneself and to become all of what one is capable of becoming.

Maslow felt that a person with unfulfilled needs low on the ladder would not be able to climb to the next step. A child's chronic pain or hunger (physical needs) or a disrupted family (lack of safety) will block the child's need for school success (self-actualization). Self-actualization is Maslow's term for a person who can manage higher needs. Self-actualizers tend to focus on problems outside themselves and have a clear sense of what is true and what is phony. They are spontaneous and creative, and for the most part, they are free of social conventions.

If we are to become self-actualizers, we must start at the bottom of the ladder. It is possible to create internal strength for dealing with unsafe conditions by finding a safe place within ourselves. Such a safe place can reduce stress and anxiety, increase relaxation, provide a safety net in emotionally challenging situations, and strengthen the capacity to draw on one's own emotional resources.

It is important to note that participants may visualize the same or different *safe place* each time they repeat this activity. Reassure participants that either experience is acceptable.

Objective: Participants will be able to use their imagery to develop an internal feeling of safety and security, reducing stress and anxiety.

Materials Needed:
Note: Two different imagery scripts

1. **Participants Grades 4–6:** Imagery script, "Making a Safe Space," "Background Music," Volume 1, track 10, or the weekly guided imagery audio *Grand Ideas from Within Counselor Edition,* Volume 1, track 8, "Making a Safe Place"
2. **Other Participants:** Imagery script "My Special Place" and "Background Music," Volume 1, track 10
3. Display weekly title and quote

Present Lesson Overview (and the age-appropriate activity):
Imagery Script:

Making a Safe Space
Grades 4–6

Day 1: Participants remain seated with background music.

1. Say, "Do not speak until directed. As you breathe in and out through your nose … closing your eyes, allow my voice to guide you … as all … other … sounds fall into the background. Becoming more relaxed … moving your attention from the outside surface of your body … and the air on your face … to your relaxing muscles … feeling more relaxed with every thought … while allowing yourself to journey inward." Pause.
2. Allow yourself to journey to a beautiful, comfortable, safe place. It may be someplace you have been before … or a place you have never seen. It could be a place in nature … a place inside a home or building … a place in fairy tales. It can be anywhere you want, anywhere at all. Just let your special space begin to take shape. If more than one place comes to mind, settle on the one that feels the most relaxing, peaceful, and safe." Pause. "This place is for you and you alone." You have one minute, which is all the

time you need to explore this special place within your mind's eye, noticing all that you see around you." Pause thirty seconds.

3. "Now begin to move your attention away from your beautiful place to the outside surface of your body … the air on your skin, the pressure of your body against the seat, and your feet on the floor … feeling relaxed, opening your eyes, being fully present and ready to work." Pause.

4. "You have two minutes to write about or draw a real picture in your journal of the imagined place you created. When you are finished, put your pencil down and sit quietly." Pause two minutes—or less if everyone is finished. "You may speak to the group."

Day 2: Participants remain seated with any relaxing music playing in the background.

1. Say, "Do not speak until directed. As you breathe in and out through your nose … closing your eyes, allow my voice to guide you … as all … other … sounds fall into the background. Becoming more relaxed … move your attention from the outside surface of your body … and the air on your face … to your relaxing muscles. Feeling more relaxed with every thought … allow yourself to journey inward." Pause.

2. "Allow yourself to journey to a beautiful, comfortable, safe place. It may be someplace you have been before … or a place you have never seen. It could be a place in nature … a place inside a home or building … a place in fairy tales. It can be anywhere you want … anywhere at all. Just let the picture begin to form. If more than one place comes to mind, or perhaps a different place from the one you discovered yesterday, settle on the one that feels the most relaxing, peaceful, and safe for you today." Pause. "This place is for you and you alone. You have one minute, which is all the time you need to explore today's special place with your ears—noticing perhaps the sounds of wind, water, or animals—hearing with your mind all the sounds of this glorious place." Pause one minute.

3. "Now begin to move your attention away from your beautiful safe place to the outside surface of your body … the air on your skin … the pressure of your body against the seat and your feet on the floor … feeling relaxed, opening your eyes, being fully present and ready to work." Pause.

4. "You have one minute to describe in your journal the sounds you hear in your special place and how they help you feel better … safe. When you finish, put your pencil down and sit quietly." Pause one minute. "You may speak to the group."

Day 3: Participants remain seated with relaxing music playing in the background.

1. Say, "Do not speak until directed. As you breathe in and out through your nose … closing your eyes, allow my voice to guide you … as all … other … sounds fall into the background. Becoming more relaxed … moving your attention from the outside surface of your body … and the air on your face … to your relaxing muscles … feeling more relaxed with every thought … allowing yourself to journey inward." Pause.

2. "Allow yourself to journey to a beautiful, comfortable, safe place. It may be someplace you have been before … or a place you have never seen. It could be a place in nature … a place inside a home or building … a place in fairy tales. It can be anywhere you want … anywhere at all. Just let the picture begin to form. If more than one place comes to mind, or perhaps a different place from the one you discovered yesterday, settle on the one that feels … the most relaxing … peaceful … and safe for you now. This place is for you and you alone." Pause.

3. "You have one minute, which is all the time you need to explore this special place through touching and sensing … noticing perhaps the texture and feel of the place where you are sitting or standing … the temperature and feel of the air on your skin … exploring your surroundings in this glorious place by touching and feeling." Pause one minute.

4. "Begin to move your attention away from your beautiful safe place to the outside surface of your body, the air on your skin, the pressure of your body against the seat, and your feet on the floor … Feeling relaxed, open your eyes, being fully present and ready to work." Pause. "You have one minute to write or draw a description of the feeling of your special place. When you are finished, put your pencil down and sit quietly." Pause one minute. "You may speak to the group."

Day 4: Participants remain seated with relaxing music playing in the background.

1. Say, "Do not speak until directed. As you breathe in and out through your nose … closing your eyes, allow my voice to guide you … as all … other … sounds fall into the background. Becoming more relaxed … move your attention from the outside surface of your body … and the air on your face … to your relaxing muscles." Pause. "Feeling more relaxed with every thought … allowing yourself to journey inward." Pause.

2. "Allow yourself to journey to a beautiful, comfortable, safe place. It may be someplace you have been before … or a place you have never seen. It could be a place in nature … a place inside a home or building … a place in fairy tales. It can be anywhere you

want … anywhere at all. Just let the picture begin to form. If more than one place comes to mind, or a different place from the one you discovered yesterday, settle on the one that feels the most relaxing, peaceful, and safe for you today. This place is for you and you alone." Pause.

3. "You have one minute, which is all the time you need to explore this special place through smell and taste … noticing perhaps the smell of flowers, or rain, or something baking, or the familiar scent of a beloved friend, pet, or object. Now notice the taste of something in this special place … maybe a refreshing beverage, a favorite food, a taste of water from a nearby stream or fruit from a nearby tree, just exploring the senses of smell and taste in this peaceful place." Pause one minute.

4. "Now begin to move your attention away from your beautiful place to the outside surface of your body … the air on your skin, the pressure of your body against the seat, and your feet on the floor … Feeling relaxed, open your eyes, being fully present and ready to work." Pause.

5. "You have one minute to describe in your journal the feelings and tastes you experienced in your special place that added to your feeling of safety. When you are finished, put your pencil down and sit quietly." Pause one minute. "You may speak to the group."

Day 5: Participants remain seated with relaxing music playing in the background.

1. Say, "Do not speak until directed. As you breathe in and out through your nose … closing your eyes, allow my voice to guide you … as all … other … sounds fall into the background. Becoming more relaxed … move your attention from the outside surface of your body … and the air on your face … to your relaxing muscles." Pause. "Feeling more relaxed with every thought … allowing yourself to journey inward … to journey to a beautiful, comfortable, safe place." Pause.

2. "It may be someplace you have been before … or a place you have never seen. It could be a place in nature … a place inside a home or building … a place in fairy tales. It can be anywhere you want … anywhere at all. Just let the picture begin to form." Pause.

3. "If more than one place comes to mind, or perhaps a different place from the one you discovered yesterday, settle on the one that feels the most relaxing, peaceful, and safe for you today. This place is for you and you alone." Pause.

4. "Explore this special place with *all* your senses … perhaps noticing the beauty around you … all that you see … and the sounds that you want to hear in your safe place … music, or wind, or water, or animals." Pause.

5. "Now, noticing what you feel here ... warmth or coolness, a gentle breeze on your skin, or textures beneath your feet." Pause. "What are you are smelling and tasting in your safe place ... the scent of a fresh spring rain or the taste of rain on your tongue, the smell and taste of a favorite food that's just come from the garden ... or out of the oven?" Pause.

6. "Sensing with all your senses what it is like to be in this glorious place." Pause thirty seconds.

7. "Now begin to move your attention away from your beautiful place to the outside surface of your body ... the air on your skin, the pressure of your body against the seat and your feet on the floor, feeling relaxed, opening your eyes, being fully present and ready to work." Pause.

For Participants in Grades 7–12+

Play audio "Background Music," Volume I track 10 (10:07), and remember to slowly read the following guided imagery script, "My Special Place." Pause to the count of five for three dots (...), the count of ten with the word *pause*, and to the count of fifteen for a *long pause*.

Imagery Script:

My Special Place
Teens to adults

1. Say, "Speak only when I direct you to do so. As you breathe in and out through your nose ... closing your eyes, allow my voice to guide you ... as all ... other ... sounds fall into the background. Becoming more relaxed ... move your attention from the outside surface of your body ... and the air on your face ... to your relaxing muscles." Pause.

2. "Feeling more relaxed with every thought [pause], allow yourself to journey inward until you come to a flight of heavy glass stairs leading down to a deeper safe level of yourself. Pausing for a moment ... you take a deep breath as you step onto the first step and notice how it creates musical sounds and illuminates in your favorite color." Pause. "Slowly taking another step down, you discover more colors and sounds ... as you take another step and another." Pause. "Journeying further and further into yourself, you arrive at a huge thick door. You know instinctively that this door protects the space on the other side—your safe place. So, you place your hand on the doorknob, turning it slowly, opening the door, and walking into a space filled with light—your safe space." Pause.

3. "Here, your space can become exactly as you like it. As your eyes adjust, you look for the important things you need—a source of light ... warmth, nourishment ... a space

to rest … a bathroom with a shower … a full-length mirror for reflecting, and pleasing nature sounds. Long pause. Add anything that is missing as you explore and create your space with your five senses." Long pause.

4. "When you are ready, find the spot in your space where you are the most comfortable and relaxed." Pause. "Becoming more relaxed, noticing again how calm … peaceful … relaxed, and safe you can feel. For one whole minute, simply allow yourself to experience the pleasure of feeling calm … safe, and relaxed in your space." Pause for one minute.

5. "And now you decide to shower as you prepare to leave this place … As you turn on the shower, you notice the water sparkles with gold … You touch the water and discover it has magical power." Pause. "You decide to stand under the water." Pause. "As each drop touches you, it illuminates all your good qualities … more and more … too many to count." Long pause.

6. "Slowly begin to move away from the golden shower of light … and prepare to leave … As you do, look in the mirror at your glowing reflection."

7. "One part of you glows more than all the rest—your gift to take with you when you leave. You turn and look around your safe space as you move toward the door. Pause. You open it and step out onto the bottom step of the illuminated glass staircase." Pause.

8. "Moving step-by-step up the colored lighted steps and through their musical sounds, your attention turns away from your safe place to the outside surface of your body … the air on your skin … the pressure of your body against the seat … and your feet on the floor. Finding yourself once again in this room, feeling calm and relaxed, open your eyes, being fully present and ready to work." Stop the music.

Verification of Participants' Understanding: Notice the participants' body language during the exercises—whether they appear restless or still. Ask for participant feedback about their *safe place*. Some participants may need reassuring that what they sense *in the mind's eye* or *imagination* may be different from how they perceive it in reality.

Note: Do not judge experiences; acknowledge that everyone has their own unique valuable experience.

Reinforce with Independent Activity: Ask participants to notice when they feel scared or angry. These are times when they can return to their internal *safe place* of peace and calm. This will enable them to deal better with the current situation.

Reassure participants that remembering to go within may be difficult initially, but ask them to attempt to remove themselves, physically or mentally, from unsafe situations by going to their internal safe place. With practice, this technique can be very effective. You may also suggest that participants do this when they are going into a scary situation, such as changes in home, work, or school.

Other Resources:

Bourne, Edmund J. 2000. *The Anxiety and Phobia Workbook, Third Edition.* New Harbinger Publications.

Naparstek, Belleruth. 2004. *Invisible Heroes: Survivors of Trauma and How They Heal.* New York: Bantam Dell, Division of Random House.

Additional Notes:

SHIFT PERCEPTIONS, SHIFT EMOTIONS

It is with the heart that one sees rightly, what is essential to the eye.

—Antoine de Saint-Exupery

Lesson 9: This lesson uses perception shifts to create the foundation for managing the four basic emotions—a foundation essential to the development of one's full potential, a satisfied self with high self-esteem.

Grade Level: 6–12-plus

Note: When presenting this lesson in one session, allow a short break between the three imagery activities

Purpose and Overview: Our first association with the feeling realm begins with the patterned emotional tones behind others' spoken words. How we say something often carries more weight than what we say or do.

Without clear inner sensations/emotions, we lose touch with who we are and what we need. Muscular tension and movement, feelings and emotions, and discomfort and well-being are all inner-world experiences. Our inner-world capacities include *proprioception* (a sense of location of body parts), *kinesthesia* (a sense of movement, weight, position, texture), and *visceral sensation* (a fullness or emptiness of digestive organs, heartbeat, pressure, pain, pleasure, sensation of thought, visual images).

Through early life experiences, our emotional patterns are framed into four basic emotions—glad, mad, sad, and afraid—that generate our perceptions of the outer world and motivate our behaviors. All emotions fall into these four basic categories. Whether *glad, mad, sad, or afraid*, our emotional state determines how others perceive us. Frequently, we are not satisfied with the reception we get.

Uninterrupted silence joined with focused concentration causes the intensity of any feeling to build—for example, a test situation. Excessive cigarette smoking, talking, and television watching serve as silence interrupters and keep an emotional condition suppressed for the moment. When others think our behaviors and emotions are unacceptable and we care about what they think, we will try to suppress our emotions through denial or displacement onto another person or animal—or by distracting ourselves from feeling the emotions, which is avoidance.

We cannot reach our full potential when any significant emotional aspect goes unexpressed in some way. All self-undermining behaviors are the result of the emotions and subsequent actions of our deprived selves.

Evidence of Self-Deprivation:
1. An inability to enjoy each moment, worrying, feeling loneliness and separateness
2. An indifference to caring statements
3. The interpretation of the actions of others
4. A focus on judging self and others
5. Action based on fear from a past experience rather than a present need
6. High incidences of conflict
7. The act of making things happen instead of allowing them to unfold

There can be various realities at the same time; everyone creates their own reality from many possibilities, which is how we are able to heal the past. As children in pain-producing situations, we first experienced fear, then sadness, followed by anger. To heal painful memories, we must travel back through these feelings in reverse order. Our left brains learn how to manage our right brains' emotional memories. Left-brained people grow toward their emotional right-brained selves, while right-brained people become more balanced by developing their intellectual selves. Whole-brain people have learned to be comfortable with their body sensations and their instincts—physical self and spiritual self are one.

Develop all four areas to become a whole-brain person.
Follow the arrows.

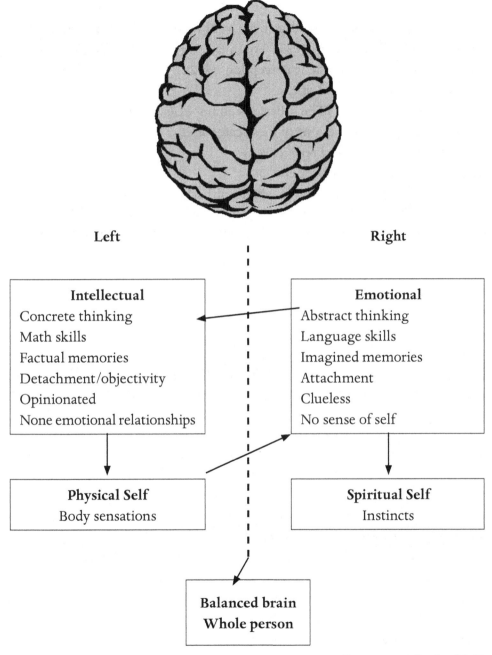

Left   Right

Intellectual
Concrete thinking
Math skills
Factual memories
Detachment/objectivity
Opinionated
None emotional relationships

Emotional
Abstract thinking
Language skills
Imagined memories
Attachment
Clueless
No sense of self

Physical Self
Body sensations

Spiritual Self
Instincts

Balanced brain
Whole person

©2011, 2020 Janice McDermott

Objective: By using mental processing techniques, participants will be able to manage their emotions when remembering.

Materials Needed:

1. Imagery script and/or Grand Ideas from Within: Audio-Guided Imagery, Volume 2, track 1, "Visual Perception" (4:35); Volume 2, track 2, "Auditory Perception" (5:52); Volume 2, track 3, "Kinesthetic Perception" (5:12).
2. Display of lesson quote and title.
3. Visual display that says, "The 4 Basic Feelings—*Glad, Mad, Sad, Afraid.*" All feeling words can be placed under one of these categories.
4. Definitions of *intensity* and *perspective.*
5. Assign each participant a partner.
6. Participants are prepared to write when finished with imagery.

Note: Redirect participants who want to talk about the content of the memory back to their *process of remembering.*

Present Lesson Overview

Read imagery script or play imagery audio, Volume 2, track 1, "Visual Perception" (4:35).

Imagery Script:

Visual Perception

Day 1: Begin with relaxing music in the background (v0lume. I. track 10.). Participants remain seated.

1. Say, "Do not speak until directed. As you breathe in and out through your nose, closing your eyes, allow all sound to fall into the background. As always, you have complete control over your imagination and are free to go wherever you like within your own mind. Now move your attention to the outside surface of your body ... the sensation of air on your hands ... neck ... face."

2. "As you continue, with eyes closed, to relax more ... breathing easily, using your mind, shift your attention to a memory of a happy time." Pause ten seconds. "You can become aware of a delightful experience and begin now to remember." Pause ten seconds. "Notice *where* in your body you can feel the happiness from this memory ... and noticing now *how* you are remembering this memory." Pause ten seconds.

3. "Is your remembering in the form of a picture … sounds … or sensations?" Pause ten seconds. "Now allow this memory to fade into the background, as another pleasant memory takes its place in foreground, and noticing again what comes first—pictures, sounds, or sensations." Pause ten seconds.

4. "Once again, breathing in and out … direct your attention toward the outside surface of your body, the air on your face, the pressure of your body against the seat … and toward my voice, remembering this: *A situation, plus what I think about it, creates how I feel.*" Pause.

5. "Now, opening your eyes, being fully present and ready to work, take thirty seconds each to share with a partner what your *experience* of remembering was like. Was it in pictures, sounds, or sensations?"

6. "When sharing your image with another person, it is important to use first-person present-tense language, to hear it aloud as though it is happening now. Use "I am" statements such as "I am walking down the yellow brick road." Share your image even when your understanding is not clear." Pause one minute. "You may speak to the group."

Note: Redirect participants who want to talk about the content of their memory back to the process of remembering.

Day 2: Participants remain seated with relaxing music in the background.

Read imagery script 0r play Audio-Guided Imagery, Volume 2, track 2, "Auditory Perception" (5:52).

Imagery Script:
Emotional Body: Glad

1. Say, "Do not speak until directed. As you breathe in and out through your nose, closing your eyes, find four sounds present in the room … Then, with only the sound of my voice guiding you, allow all those sounds to fall into the background. As you continue to breathe with eyes closed … begin at your feet to scan your body. Notice any tension and hold it, tighter, tighter, and release, relaxing, and continuing in this way up through your body." Pause. "Becoming more relaxed as you journey through your body until you are still, still as a lake." Long pause.

2. "Using your mind, shift your attention inward." Pause. "Now recall a familiar pleasant memory … any happy memory will do … and notice where in your body you feel

happy, glad." Pause. "If your pleasant memory is in color, notice what happens to your *glad* feeling when you change it to black and white." Pause. "If your pleasant memory is black and white, change it to color. Pause. "Again, notice what happens to your *glad* feeling." Pause.

3. "This time notice if you are *seeing* yourself in your memory or ... are you *feeling* yourself, *experiencing* your memory? Pause. "Notice when you are in your memory that you can touch and feel the things you see around you. Pause. "Also notice how much happier you can feel when being in the memory *feeling* ... as compared to simply *watching* your memory." Long pause.

4. "Now ... return your memory to its original form, the way it was when you started." Pause. "If your original pleasant memory is a photograph, turn it into a movie ... and if it is a movie, turn it into a photograph. Notice the change in your feeling." Long pause.

5. "Discover something new in your memory and notice what happens to your happy feeling." Pause. "You may want to remember this information about yourself for later or not." Pause.

6. "Now, directing your attention to the outside surface of your body ... notice again the sensation of air on your face. Using your mind, shift your attention toward my voice and open your eyes ... being fully present and ready to work. Take thirty seconds to record when your feeling gets more intense." Pause thirty seconds.

7. "Do they get stronger when your memory is moving or still?" Pause.

8. "When in black and white or color?" Pause.

9. "When close or far away?" Pause.

10. "Does your emotion get stronger when you are in the memory or when you are watching yourself in your memory?" Pause thirty seconds. "You may speak to the group."

Emotional Body: Mad

Day 3: Participants remain seated with relaxing music, Volume 1, track 10, playing in the background—or play Volume 2, track 3, "Kinesthetic Perception" (5:12).

1. Say, "Do not speak until directed. As you breathe in and out through your nose ... closing your eyes ... identify four sounds as they fall into the background ... Allow my voice to guide you. As you continue to breathe with eyes closed, begin at your feet to scan your body ... noticing any tension and tightening more." Pause. "Releasing, relaxing ... and continuing up your body ... becoming more relaxed with every thought." Long pause. "Using your mind, shift your attention inward." Pause.

2. "You know ... you have a certain difficulty in your life ... that you would like to bring to a satisfactory resolution ... maybe a *mad* memory, one that causes your body to become tense and your heart to beat a little faster, one you have been trying to keep in the background so you won't lose your temper." Pause.

3. "When you find it, notice where in your body you can feel angry, where you are mad." Pause ten seconds. "Turn down the Volume of the words in your *mad* memory to a whisper ... and notice your body change." Pause. "Return the volume to its original level."

4. "Now change the rhythm of the words to sound like Donald Duck talking." Pause. "Again, what happens to your body sensation?"

5. "Return your *mad* memory to its original form ... This time take your mad memory and slooow ... it ... dooown ... and ... notice ... 0the level ... of feeling ... when sound ... is very ... slooow." Long pause.

6. "You may choose to change your feeling connected with this memory by turning down the sound or changing the speed or rhythm. You are in charge of this feeling. No one can make you feel. You do it by the way you choose to think." Long pause.

7. "Now, directing your attention to the outside surface of your body ... return your attention to the sensation of air on your face." Pause. "Using your mind, shift your attention toward my voice ... opening your eyes ... being fully present and ready to work."

8. Take thirty seconds to record which way changing *memory words* causes your *mad* feeling to be less intense. Does your mad feeling become less by changing volume, speed, rhythm?" Pause thirty seconds for writing. "You may speak to the group. Are there any questions?"

Kinesthesia Body: Sad

Day 4: Begin with relaxing music in the background. Participants remain seated.

1. Say, "Do not speak until directed. As you breathe in and out through your nose, closing your eyes, allow all sound to fall into the background." Pause.

2. "As you continue to breathe, begin scanning your body for tension, starting at your feet ... tightening more any tense muscles ... and releasing, relaxing, and continuing upward ... tightening and relaxing ... becoming more relaxed with every thought." Long pause.

3. Using your mind, shift your attention inward to a certain difficulty in your life that you want to bring to a satisfactory resolution, perhaps this time a *sad* memory. Find

a visual memory of this *sad* feeling." Pause. "Where in your body do you feel sad?" Pause ten seconds.

4. "Remember, if you are in the memory, you are intensifying your sad feeling, making it stronger, sadder, and even sadder." Pause. "Notice that your *sad* feeling can fade as you choose to step back ... out of the memory, looking at it." Pause.

5. "Now try pushing this sad memory picture way out in front of you until it is the size of a postage stamp." Pause. "Change memory to black and white ... Place it in an envelope and mail it far away." Pause. "Watch this memory fade into the background. Say goodbye as your *sad* feeling leaves your body." Pause.

6. "Now give yourself a mental treat for all your hard work, find another *glad* memory ... and make the necessary adjustments—getting into the picture to intensify the feeling of *glad* until it fills up your whole body, spilling out into the world, creating even more and more happiness everywhere." Long pause.

7. "Now shift your attention toward my voice and, using your mind, remember this: "To change a feeling ... change the Volume ... the speed or rhythm of words ... or change the color ... size or perspective of a memory picture." Long pause.

8. "Moving your attention to the outside surface of your body ... the air on your face and the pressure of your body against the seat, feeling relaxed; open your eyes, being fully present and ready to work." Pause. "Take thirty seconds to record how you can make your *sad* feeling feel less sad. Is it when your memory is moving or still ... in color or black and white ... close up or far away?" Pause thirty seconds. "You may speak to the group."

Culmination

Day 5: Participants remain seated with relaxing music in the background.

1. Say, "Do not speak until directed. As you breathe in and out through your nose, closing your eyes, allow all sounds to fall into the background as my voice guides you." Pause. "As you continue to breathe with eyes closed, beginning at your feet, scan your body." Pause. "Notice any tension and tighten more ... Release, relax, and continue up your body, tightening more and relaxing ... until you are completely relaxed." Long pause.

2. "Using your mind, shift your attention inward." Pause. "Becoming more relaxed with every thought and using the information you have learned about the process of change, change your inner experience to an outstandingly happier one." Long pause.

3. "Remember that loud volume and a close-up picture increases any of your four feelings." Pause. "Allow any memory to be in the foreground … managing it in any way … making this moment more enjoyable or not." Pause one minute.

4. "Feeling relaxed and confidant in your ability to manage your feelings by using your mind, shift your attention toward my voice and remember this: To change a *feeling*, change the words … Volume, speed, or rhythm." Pause. "To change a feeling, an emotion, change the picture's color, size, and/or perspective." Pause.

5. "Now direct your attention to the outside surface of your body … the sensation of air on your face and your body in the room." Pause. "Now open your eyes, being present, looking with soft eyes at others around you."

Verification of Participants' Understanding: Ask the following questions:

1. What are the four basic feelings? (glad, mad, sad, afraid)
2. How do you change the words you hear in a memory? (change Volume, slow speed, or interrupt rhythm)
3. How can you now change a remembered past vent or an imagined future scene event to create more or less feeling? (Change color to black and white, big to small, near to far; change perspective: in to out, moving to still, or change the content.)

Reinforce with Independent Activity:
Session 1: Have participants share with a family member this technique for managing feelings and then report back.

Session 2: Have participants describe how this technique could help when feeling afraid or anxious about a test, a speech, or job interview.

Session 3:
1. Have participants repeat all the vowel sounds—*aaaaa* (glad), *eeeee* (afraid), *iiiii* (mad), *ooooo* (sad), *uuuuu* (glad)—after you with an extended sound and an emotional inflection: glad, afraid, mad, sad, and glad again.
2. Ask participants to draw two pictures, one of an intensified feeling and another of the feeling diminished.
3. Ask participants to describe a situation in which their thinking caused them to feel *mad* or *sad* to identify what new information they used to change what they were thinking, hence changing feeling. Through which of the five senses did the new information come?

Other Resources:

Brewer, Chris and Campbell, Don G. 1991. *Rhythms of Learning.* Tucson: Zephry Press.

Grinder, John and Bandler, Richard. 1981. *Trance-formations.* Moah: Real People Press.

Jacobson, Sid, 1986. *Meta-cation, Volume I. II. III*, P. Berkley: Meta Publications.

Additional Notes:

ANCHORING WITH TRANSITIONAL OBJECTS

Happiness does not depend on outward things, but on the way, we see them.

—Count Leo Tolstoy

Lesson 10: Diminishing Anxiety, Embracing the Future

Grade Level: 4–12-plus

Note: Best done in two or three sessions

Purpose and Overview: The human psyche seems to mark time much like a tree—a ring for every year—for inside each of us is the person we were for each year of our life. Regardless of our age, our experiences before the age of six continue to influence our current choices. The young children in us believe in the possibility of the impossible and, regardless of biological age, appreciate a concrete transitional object when moving from a point of security to a less safe situation. Our transitional object helps us see and hear from our world within.

A transitional object can be any object that serves as a bridge between something we leave behind and something toward which we move. When a child begins to separate from the mother, he chooses an object to replace her—a baby blanket or stuffed animal that reminds him of his mother. The transitional object supports the child in expressing his autonomy. This process of bringing a piece of the past into the new continues even into adulthood. We call our transitional objects amulets, lucky charms, talismans, or mascots.

Adults often place their sensory awareness into the background and use a transitional object such as a crystal, a washed stone, a prayer shawl, a rosary, or a cross to help shift into a feeling or place we want to experience again. Some of us use our cell phones as our transitional object. Others use their intuition to quickly make their shift from outside to inside without a transitional object.

As we practice and become more comfortable with ourselves in this process, we can give up the *actual* object for the *imagined* transitional object. We imagine the feel of the rock, the sound of the drum, the sight of the cross, or the sound or feel of our own breath to help us feel safe as we transition to the inner state of meditation or prayer.

What are the transitional objects in your house and where have you placed them? Do they connect the past to the present, the physical to the spiritual, or the living to the dead?

When you imagine the future, what component of the present serves as your bridge—an image of your house, car, a location, or a body sensation? Do you first think how these things are now, and then how you would like them to be in the future? Are you taking action to make changes or are you stopping yourself with your fears?

Sometimes we hold on to our experiences through fear, re-creating what we fear in an attempt to justify our pasts. We make statements such as, "See, I knew I couldn't pass that test" or "I was afraid that would happen." Our future depends on us—our thoughts, our dreams and our actions. Sometimes moving toward future success is too scary. A transitional object, to connect the security of *now* to the uncertainty of *then*, may be all we need.

Objective: While studying, participants will use a transitional object to anchor learning and to strengthen confidence. They will use the same object for recall during an exam on the materials studied and to have a challenging conversation or job interview.

Materials Needed:
1. Imagery script and Grand Ideas from Within Counselor Edition, Volume 1, track 10; "Background Music" or Grand Ideas from Within Counselor Edition: Audio-Guided Imagery, Volume 2, track 4, "Anchoring Power" (5:18); track 5, "Anchoring Transitions" (5:43), and track 6, "Anchoring Success" (4:28).
2. A display of the weekly title, quote, and the following definition. A transitional object is any object that connects people, places, or events—for example, baby blanket, teddy bear, rabbit's foot, stone.
3. Any small object from the participants' desk or person—paper clip, eraser, pen, ring— the same or similar object to be used each session.
4. A designated person with whom to share (optional).

Present Lesson Overview:
Read imagery script with "Background Music" or play audio, Volume 2, track 4.

Note: Participants sit erect with eyes closed while holding their selected object in their *nondominant* hand.

Imagery Script:

Anchoring Power

Day 1: Say, "Do not speak until directed. As you breathe in and out through your nose, closing your eyes, allow my voice to guide you ... as all other ... sounds fall ... into the background."

1. "As you continue with your eyes closed ... to relax more ... you know you have complete control over your imagination and are free to go wherever you like within your own mind. Now move your attention from the outside surface of your body ... the air on your face ... your relaxing muscles, to the object you are holding ... feeling more relaxed with every thought, you and your object journey inward." Pause ten seconds.

2. "Inside yourself, feel the object's surfaces—the texture, the firmness, the shape." Pause. "Allow a colored image of your object to come to mind." Pause. "Now create a scene, the beginning of a magical story that goes like this:
"Once upon a time in life ... the heavens sprinkled an invisible powerful cosmic dust over the whole world. This dust fell on living creatures ... and all ... their treasured objects." Pause. "Only the living creatures ... with the ability to travel inward could use the hidden power available to them. Some did, and others did not. Even when others hear of the magic available to them, they choose not to believe it. Nevertheless ... those who dare to relax ... and travel inward ... soon discover the confidence needed for remembering ... remembering all they have studied and learned in the moment necessary for their success." Pause. "Once we use this power of connecting knowledge with objects, it becomes a memory key ... forever available ... when needed, even now." Pause.

3. "As you feel the object you are holding, you can create a scene from the future of your life, a scene where you are required to recall important information." Pause. "Notice the colors ... sounds ... and smells of this inner space." Pause. "Rubbing your object, release the information needed into your mind ... and move forward in the scene to your moment of success ... feeling in your body the pleasure of working with your powers within ... and knowing how to create this moment again and again." Pause thirty seconds.

4. Moving your attention to the outside surface of your body … the air on your face and the pressure of your body against the seat, feeling relaxed; open your eyes, being fully present and ready to work." Pause.

5. "Take thirty seconds to share with a partner your feeling of success, and its location in your body. Did your success scene have color, sound, movement? If not, what can you imagine would change by adding these components? You may speak to your designated partner."

Read following imagery script, "Anchoring Transitions," while playing Volume 1, track 10, "Background Music," or play audio script, Volume 2, track 5, "Anchoring Transitions."

Imagery Script:

Anchoring Transitions

Day 2: Participants remain seated and holding previous day's selected object in the nondominant hand. Begin with relaxing music playing in the background.

1. Say, "Do not speak until directed. As you hold your object in your nondominant hand, breathe in and out through your nose … closing your eyes; allow my voice to guide you … as … all … other … sounds fall into the background." Pause. "Moving your attention from the outside surface of your body, the air on your face, your relaxing muscles, to the object you are holding, feeling more relaxed with every thought … you and your object … journey inward." Pause.

2. "Inside yourself, feel the object's surfaces—the texture … the firmness … the shape." Pause. "Allow a colored image of your object to come to mind." Pause. "Now create a scene, the beginning of a magical story that goes like this: *Once upon a time in life, the heavens sprinkled an invisible powerful cosmic dust over the whole world. This dust fell on living creatures and all their treasured objects. Only the living creatures with the ability to travel inward could use the hidden power available to them. Some did, and others did not. Even when others heard of the magic available to them, they chose not to believe it. Nevertheless, those who dare to relax and travel inward … soon discover the confidence needed for remembering all they have studied and learned in the moment, necessary for their success."* Pause. "Once this power of connecting knowledge with objects is used, it becomes a memory key … forever available … when needed." Long pause.

3. "Now, as you feel the object you are holding, create a scene from your own life's future—a colorful scene of you walking toward a seat … holding your transitional object in one hand and your writing instrument in the other, and then sitting down."

Pause. "You notice, as you look at the questions ... how easy it is to read and understand when your mind uses your transitional object as a memory key to your deeper ... resources ... and skills, enabling you to recall the important required information." Pause. "Rubbing your object, you release the information you need into your mind." Pause. "Notice the colors ... sounds and smells of this inner space." Pause.

4. "And moving forward in the scene to the moment of success ... feel in your body the pleasure of working with your powers within and knowing how to create this moment again and again." Long pause.

5. "Moving your attention to the outside surface of your body ... the air on your face and the pressure of your body against the seat, feeling relaxed ... open your eyes, being fully present and ready to work." Pause.

6. "Now take thirty seconds to remember your feeling of success and its location in your body." Pause thirty seconds. "Compare your experience to yesterday's." Pause thirty seconds. "Are there any questions or comments? You may speak."

Read imagery script "Anchoring Success" while playing Volume 1, track 10, "Background Music," or play audio script, Volume 2, track 6, "Anchoring Success."

Note: This lesson is repeated to strengthen the power in using a transitional object.

Imagery Script:

Anchoring Success

Days 3–5: Participants remain seated, holding selected object in the nondominant hand with relaxing music playing in the background.

1. Say, "Do not speak until directed. As you breathe in and out through your nose, closing your eyes, allow my voice to guide you as all ... other ... sounds ... fall into the background. Following your attention from the outside surface of your body ... the air on your face and hands ... to muscles relaxing, and to the object you are holding in your nondominant hand ... feeling more relaxed with every thought ... you and your object may now journey inward." Pause.

2. "Traveling at the speed of light through your future years, catching quick looks at your life's successes that are creating as you travel ... you are impressed with the wonders of yourself." Pause. "Feel yourself grow through your talents ... your unique gifts and skills and practices ... and becoming a bigger, fuller, even more successful self. Pause for one minute—all the time in the world—and enjoy your successful life." Pause one minute.

3. "Now traveling at the speed of light, travel in time to this present moment, moving your attention to the outside surface of your body ... the air on your face and the pressure of your body against the seat. Feeling relaxed." Pause, noticing participants return to physical awareness before speaking. "Open your eyes, being fully present and ready to work." Pause.

4. "Take fifteen seconds to remember your feeling of success and its location in your body." Pause fifteen seconds. "Compare your experience to yesterday's." Pause fifteen seconds. "Are there any questions or comments? You may speak."

Note: Participants may not be able to remember any of this exercise on a conscious level. If they report sleeping, simply reply, "That must be what you needed. Nevertheless, some part of you was listening."

Verification of Participants' Understanding:
Session 1: Ask, "What object did you select as your talisman?" Check to be sure that the selected object is suitable and allowed during test taking.

Session 2: Ask, "Did you remember to take your object inward?"

Session 3: Ask, "What are some characteristics of your success?"

Reinforce with Independent Activity: Use the terms *amulet, lucky charm, talisman, and mascot* for a word study or spelling assignment. Conduct an experiment in the group by having participants select a personal object that is available both at home and at school to use while studying or doing homework and again when being tested on the same material. For those who do well on the tested material, ask, "Which of you used a transitional object—and how did it help you?" Encourage participants to use the same object for a whole unit of study and compare the results.

Other Resources:
Grolnick, Simon A; Barkin, Leonard; Muensterberger, Werner. 1978. *Between Reality and Fantasy: Transitional Objects and Phenomena*, New York: J. Aronson.

EXPLORING MY WORLD

We make ourselves either happy or miserable. The amount of work is the same.

—Carlos Castaneda

Lesson 11: Developing a Positive Perspective on Life

Grade Level: 4–12-plus

Purpose and Overview: Each of us, for some portion of time—and often for large portions of time—focuses on the negative aspects of our lives rather than the positive. Additionally, there may be a significant aspect of our lives that we take for granted, fail to notice, or fail to appreciate. Some of us assume we will always have food to eat or heat in our homes, and we fail to appreciate the blessing of enough. A teacher, neighbor, or friend may nurture a child whose birth family is not emotionally or physically supportive, yet the child devalues the gift because the givers are not family.

When we explore an imaginary world through the mind's eye and focus on its positive aspects, we bring a more positive outlook into our physical world, creating a more fulfilling reality as well.

Objective: Through imagery exercises, participants will be able to notice more sensory details and incorporate them into writing, artwork, and oral expression of appreciation and gratitude.

Materials Needed:
1. Grand Ideas from Within Counselor Edition, Volume 1, track 10, "Background Music," or Volume 1, track 9, "Exploring My World" (7:25)
2. Display of weekly title and quote
3. Paper, and pencil or markers

Present Lesson Overview:
Read guided imagery scripts while playing Volume 1, track 10, "Background Music."

Weekly Group: Play Volume 1, track 9, "Exploring My World" (7:25).

Imagery Script:

Exploring My World

Day 1: Participants remain seated. Begin with relaxing music playing in the background.

1. Say, "Do not speak until directed. As you breathe in and out through your nose ... closing your eyes, allow my voice to guide you ... as all ... other ... sounds fall into the background ... as you continue, with eyes closed, to relax more." Pause. "You know you have complete control over your imagination and are free to go wherever you like within your own mind. Becoming more relaxed ... move your attention from the outside surface of your body ... and the air on your face ... to your relaxing muscles ... feeling more relaxed with every thought ... allowing yourself to journey inward." Pause.

2. "Imagine climbing aboard a colorful carpet for a trip around your world. Your carpet is of your special design and color for this trip ... and it is a delightful and safe way to travel." Pause. "You feel a gentle wind on your face as you rise into the air high above the earth ... looking down upon the meadows and mountains ... rivers and oceans ... noticing a country you'd like to explore. Directing your carpet to land there, you take in the sights ... and smells ... and sounds ... of this place." Pause.

3. "A protector appears and helps you from your carpet, informing you that you have landed in the country of kindred spirits. The protector waves his hand, surrounding you with a soft invisible light shield, which allows you to take in whatever feelings you wish ... and protects you from what you don't want or need." Pause. "As you tingle with excitement and anticipation, the protector waves the wand again, drawing from all directions your kindred spirits—those family members ... friends ... teachers ... ancestors ... animals, or angels who love, nurture, and support you in one way or another." Pause.

4. "You may not recognize some of those who are present. Some of those you see may even surprise you. Trusting that you are safe and protected, and that the protector has brought only that which is positive for you, take a moment to feel the caring of those around you ... noticing that different beings love and nurture you in different ways." Pause one minute.

5. "Feeling peaceful, protected, and calm, you move back onto your carpet ... bidding goodbye to the protector and your kindred spirits. As you gently rise into the air ... traveling safely, and at the speed of light, back to this present moment ... moving your

attention to the outside surface of your body, the air on your face … and the pressure of your body against the seat, feeling relaxed, open your eyes, being fully present and ready to work." Pause.

6. "Now, breathing easily and naturally, take a moment to write or draw about your experience. When you are finished, put your pencil down and sit quietly." Pause one minute. "You may speak."

Day 2: Participants remain seated with relaxing music playing in the background.

1. Say, "Do not speak until directed. As you breathe in and out through your nose … closing your eyes, allow my voice to guide you … as all other … sounds fall into the background. Becoming more relaxed … move your attention from the outside surface of your body … and the air on your face … to your relaxing muscles." Pause. "Feeling more relaxed with every thought … allow yourself to journey inward." Pause.

2. "Imagine again climbing aboard your special carpet for a trip around your world. Your carpet is of your special design and color, and it is a delightful and safe way to travel." Pause. Feeling a gentle wind on your face as you rise into the air high above the earth … looking down upon the meadows and mountains … rivers and oceans … noticing a place you would like to explore. Directing your carpet to land there … and as it does … taking in the sights … smells, sounds, and feeling of the place." Pause. "The protector, helping you from your carpet, informs you that you have landed in the place of knowledge and understanding." Pause.

3. "The protector waves a hand … and surrounds you with a soft … invisible … light shield, allowing you to take in whatever feelings are important to your learning and protecting you from what you don't want or need." Pause. "And as you tingle with excitement and anticipation, the protector motions you to follow down the path of wisdom … allowing you to see and understand the knowledge that is available to you now and in the future." Pause.

4. "Trusting that you are safe and protected, you eagerly observe your opportunities for learning … seeing the positive aspects in some of the knowledge that is difficult for you now. You may see a parent teaching you to drive a car … or a friend teaching you a game … maybe a sibling teaching you a sport … or a teacher exploring a new subject with you … possibly a chef teaching you to cook … or an artisan teaching you a skill. Knowing that this protector has brought only that which is positive for you, take a moment to absorb the joy and observe the opportunities for learning in your world." Pause one minute.

5. "Feeling peaceful, protected, and calm, you move back onto your carpet … bidding goodbye to the protector and feeling thankful for your understanding … as you gently rise into the air. Traveling safely, and at the speed of light, to this present moment, you move your attention to the outside surface of your body … the air on your face … and the pressure of your body against the seat, feeling relaxed … Open your eyes, being present and ready to work." Pause.

6. "Breathing easily and naturally, take a minute to write or draw about your experience. When you are finished, put your pencil down and sit quietly." Pause one minute. "You may speak to the group."

Day 3: Participants remain seated with relaxing music playing in the background.

1. Say, "Do not speak until directed. As you breathe in and out through your nose … closing your eyes, allow my voice to guide you … as all … other … sounds fall into the background." Pause. "Becoming more relaxed … moving your attention from the outside surface of your body … and the air on your face … to your relaxing muscles … feeling more relaxed with every thought … allowing yourself to journey inward." Pause.

2. "Imagine climbing aboard your trusty carpet for a trip around your world. Your carpet is of your special design and color, and it is a delightful and safe way to travel. Feeling a gentle wind on your face as you rise into the air high above the earth … looking down upon the meadows and mountains … rivers and oceans … noticing a place you would like to explore. Directing your carpet to land there … and as it does … taking in the sights … and smells and sounds … and feelings of the place." Pause. "A protector, who informs you that you have landed on Fun Island, helps you from your carpet."

3. "The protector waves a hand, surrounding you with a soft invisible shield, which allows you to take in whatever feelings are important to your learning and protects you from what you do not want or need. Trusting that you are safe and protected, and that the protector has brought only that which is positive for you … you tingle with excitement and anticipation." Pause. "The protector motions for you to run freely about the island … exploring and experiencing all the things you have ever done or wanted to do to satisfy your playful self and relieve the stress in your world. Take a moment to play on Fun Island." Pause one minute.

4. "Feeling peaceful … protected and calm, you move back onto your carpet, bidding goodbye to the protector and feeling thankful for your understanding as you gently rise into the air." Pause. "Traveling safely, and at the speed of light, to this present

moment … you move your attention to the outside surface of your body … the air on your face … and the pressure of your body against the seat. Feeling relaxed … open your eyes, being fully present and ready to work." Pause.

5. "Now, breathing easily and naturally, take one minute to write about or draw your experience. When you are finished, put your pencil down and sit quietly." Pause one minute. "You may speak to the group."

Day 4: Participants remain seated with relaxing music playing in the background.

1. Say, "Do not speak until directed. As you breathe in and out through your nose … closing your eyes, allow my voice to guide you … as all … other … sounds fall into the background. Becoming more relaxed … move your attention from the outside surface of your body … and the air on your face … to your relaxing muscles." Pause. "Feeling more relaxed with every thought … allow yourself to journey inward." Pause.

2. "Imagine climbing aboard your carpet for a trip around your world. Your carpet is of your special design and color for this trip, and it is a delightful and safe way to travel. Feeling a gentle wind on your face as you rise into the air high above the earth, you look down upon the meadows and mountains, rivers and oceans, taking in the sights … smells … sounds … and feelings of this place." Pause. "And as you do, you notice a cave that you'd like to explore beneath a tall and stately mountain. You direct your carpet to land there … and your protector helps you from your carpet, informing you that you have landed at the Cave of Magnificent Mountain." Pause.

3. "You pause for a moment … perhaps fearful of the dark or unknown … but the protector waves a hand, surrounding you with a soft invisible light shield, which allows you to take in whatever is important to your learning and protects you from what you don't want or need. And as you tingle with excitement and anticipation, the protector motions for you to walk together. You sense the warm presence of the protector beside you as you enter the cave together."

4. "Adjusting your eyes to the darkness, you both walk down a damp and rocky path … going deeper and deeper into the mountain. Though the path is difficult and you stumble along the way, the protector keeps you from falling … and directs you toward a dim light ahead in another part of the cave. As you approach the source of the light, it becomes brighter, drawing you into the deepest part of the cave … into the chamber of light."

5. "The protector enters first, and you follow. Entering this space, alive with sparkling white energy, you are surprised and delighted to discover a room full of treasures. The

protector motions for you to explore it all—touching, feeling, smelling, and tasting all that you see. Remembering that you are safe and protected, and that the protector only brings that which is positive for you, you take a moment to explore all of these treasures within." Pause fifteen seconds.

6. "Feeling peaceful, protected, and calm … knowing that you can return to this place anytime you wish … you leave the Cave of Magnificent Mountain, moving back onto your carpet, bidding goodbye to the protector … and gently rise into the air."

7. "Traveling safely and at the speed of light to this present moment, moving your attention to the outside surface of your body, the air on your face and the pressure of your body against the seat, feeling relaxed … opening your eyes, being fully present and ready to work." Pause.

8. "Continuing to breathe easily and naturally, take a minute to write or draw about your experience. When you are finished, put your pencil down and sit quietly." Pause one minute. "You may speak to the group."

Day 5: Participants remain seated with relaxing music playing in the background.

1. Say, "Do not speak until directed. As you breathe in and out through your nose … closing your eyes, allow my voice to guide you as all … other … sounds fall into the background." Pause. "Becoming more relaxed … move your attention from the outside surface of your body … and the air on your face … to your relaxing muscles." Pause. "Feeling more relaxed with every thought … allow yourself to journey inward." Pause.

2. "Imagine climbing aboard your trusty carpet, once more a delightful and safe way to travel, for one last trip around your world. Feeling the familiar gentle wind on your face as you rise into the air high above the earth … looking down upon the meadows and mountains … rivers and oceans … as they fade away, your carpet climbing higher and higher." Pause.

3. "Moving through the clouds, feeling a familiar warm, protective presence by your side … you turn to see that the protector has joined you for this ride." Pause. "Once again … with the wave of a hand … a soft invisible light shield surrounds you, which allows you to take in whatever is important to your learning, protecting you from what you do not want or need. Trusting that you are safe and protected, and that the protector has brought only that which is positive for you, you begin to tingle with excitement and anticipation." Pause.

4. "The protector tells you that you have all the time in the world to enjoy, with all of your senses, the sun ... the moon ... the stars ... the planets ... and all the wonders of the sky, and so you do." Pause one minute.

5. "Feeling peaceful, protected, calm, and knowing that you can return to this place anytime you wish ... you direct your carpet homeward. Bidding goodbye to the protector ... and traveling safely at the speed of light ... you return to this present moment."

6. "Moving your attention to the outside surface of your body, and the air on your face ... and the pressure of your body against the seat, you can feel relaxed." Pause. "Open your eyes, being present and ready to work." Pause.

7. "Now, breathing easily and naturally, take a moment to write, using statements that begin with *I*, or draw about your experience, including yourself in the picture. When you are finished, put your pencil down and sit quietly." Pause one minute. "You may speak to the group."

Verification of Participants' Understanding: information in journal that indicates an elaboration of the subject matter mentioned in the imagery exercises

Reinforce with Independent Activity: Have participants use all their senses to explore and perhaps write about different activities experienced throughout the school or workday. Have them describe the small details observed during activities, a test, at lunch, and during break time, comparing the different feelings created by their experiences.

Other Resources:
Davis, Martha and Eshelman, Elizabeth Robbins, McKay, Matthew. 1995. *The Relaxation and Stress Reduction Workbook, Fourth Edition.* Oakland: New Harbinger Publications.

Additional Notes:

LESSONS 12–13
PSYCHOLOGICAL AND SOCIAL NEEDS

ACCEPTANCE, BELONGING, LOVE

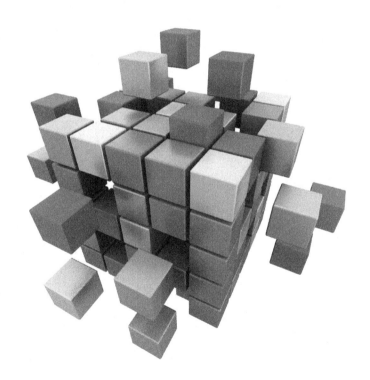

MENDING WHAT'S BROKEN

Stop thinking in terms of limitations and start thinking in terms of possibilities.

—Terry Josephson

Lesson 12: Improving Self-Concept

Grade Level: 6–12-plus

Note: Allow a significant break between imagery activities.

Purpose and Overview: This week's activities provide ways to use the materials learned thus far in a more complex and success-oriented way. We all can have thoughts that cause us to hesitate or be reticent rather than utilize our talents and move more quickly toward success. *Hesitancy* is created by thoughts that suggest a lack of something within the individual, such as "I don't know enough," "I'm not good enough," or "I'm afraid."

Reticence, on the other hand, expresses a desire without the permission needed for pursuit, such as, "That would be fun to do, but my friends won't like it" or "I would like to go to college, but no one else in my family has gone." Reticence consumes time and slows success.

A participant creates *hesitancy* when reminded four or five times of his failures. He begins to generalize, applies the generalization to himself, and believes he is a failure, not capable of succeeding. This limiting belief becomes part of his self-concept.

These imagery exercises ask the participant to identify a limiting personal belief that causes hesitancy, a disliked belief that would allow more choices if discarded—for example, "I am stupid." Since every thought is composed of our senses, it can be taken apart sense by sense. (1) What is the *limiting* thought's visual components—is it close or far away, black and white, or in color? Is it moving or still? (2) The participant identifies a self-enhancing *belief he* can use to move closer to success—for example, "I can succeed at anything when I stick with it." What is the belief's visual components—is the memory close or far away, black and white, or in color? Is it moving or still? Again, there should be one or more sensory differences. Finally, the participant uses this information to begin to change the unwanted limiting belief.

Objective: Participants will experience ways to change *self-limiting* thinking to *possibility* thinking and develop patience in using their own minds as resources for information.

Materials Needed:
1. Imagery script and Grand Ideas from Within Counselor Edition Volume 1, track 10, "Background Music," or audio-guided imageries, Volume 2, track 7, "Limitations" (6:03); track 8, "Enhancements" (5:23); track 9, "Abundance" (6:03)
2. A display of chapter quotes and sensory components:
   a) Close or far away
   b) Black and white or in color
   c) Moving or still
3. Writing materials
4. One copy of appendix "Image Component Comparison List" (use the same one each session)

Present Lesson Overview (and read or play imagery activities):
Imagery Script:

Mending What's Broken

Day 1: Limitations: Participants remain seated, writing materials, a copy of appendix "Image Component," pencil on desk, and relaxing music in the background.

1. Say, "Do not speak until directed. We will begin an information-gathering journey. As you softly breathe in and out through your nose … closing your eyes … allowing my voice to guide you … as all other sounds fall … into the background. As you continue, with eyes closed, to relax more … you know you have complete control over your imagination and are free to go wherever you like within your own mind." Becoming more relaxed … move your attention from the outside surface of your body to your relaxing muscles." Pause. "Feeling yourself relaxing … even more … relaxed with every thought, you journey inward … deep inside, where all truth resides." Pause.
2. "You are able to find a place of peace and wisdom here. From this place of wisdom, you search and find a statement that makes you think you somehow are *incomplete* … something missing in you." Pause. "And if this missing something could be available, it would make your life better; maybe you could spell or multiply correctly … You

could ... make better grades, speak up for yourself, have more success, and follow your dream." Pause. "There may be many times when you could use this missing part ... and so you accept it and form a thought around it ... a statement about yourself that you can believe to be true." Pause.

3. "Notice that when you put all these times that you have a limiting belief about yourself together, you can easily complete the sentence "I am ...," or the sentence "I need to be more ...," or I have to ..." Pause. "Find your one sentence that describes your limitation." Pause. "Even though others tell you your negative statement about yourself is not true, you notice that you keep finding proof otherwise."

4. "Now in your wisdom place, you can decide to do something different, to use your wisdom to investigate your limiting sentence by noticing the visual components of your one-sentence belief." Pause.

5. "Draw a picture in your mind of this belief or make it a photograph or a movie, whichever you prefer." Pause. "Then notice if it is moving or still." Pause. "If it is in color or black and white." Pause. "If it is close or far away." Pause. "Are you looking at this belief or are you in it?" Pause thirty seconds.

6. "Bringing all this information back to this moment, move your attention to the outside surface of your body ... the pressure of your body against your seat ... and the air on your face ... feeling relaxed ... open your eyes, being fully present and ready to work." Pause.

7. "Using your worksheet, write your *limiting* sentence on the first line." Allow time to write. "Now list its components below." Allow time to write. "You may speak to the group. Are there any questions?"

Day 2: No Difference: Participants remain seated with writing materials—"Image Component" page and pencil—on desk and relaxing music in the background.

1. Say, "Do not speak until directed. As you softly breathe in and out through your nose ... breathing in ... and out ... in ... and out ... closing your eyes ... breathing easily, allowing my voice to guide you ... as all ... other sounds ... fall ... into the background, the sounds of the movement, of breathing, of thinking falling into the background."

2. "Focusing on the sound of my voice, becoming more relaxed ... moving your attention from the outside surface of your body ... to your relaxing muscles ... feeling yourself relaxing even more." Relaxing now with every thought ... as you journey inward." Pause.

3. "From here, you recall a simple recent decision where the outcome made no real difference in your life ... like choosing a vanilla or strawberry shake ... choosing to buy a yellow or red notebook, or choosing to wear a green or blue shirt. Recall only one decision like this ... one you have already made."

4. "Now, with this decision in mind, notice its components. Is it moving or still?" Pause. "Is it in color or black and white? Pause. "Is it close or far away?" Pause. "Are you looking at it or are you in it?" Pause.

5. "Coming back to this present moment, moving your attention to the outside surface of your body ... the pressure of your body against the seat, and the air on your face ... feeling relaxed ... open your eyes, being fully present and ready to work." Pause.

6. "On your worksheet, check the components of your simple decision labeled *No Difference*. There is no sentence for this column." Allow time for writing. "Underline the components that are different from column one. There may be only one. Allow time for writing. "You may speak to the group. Are there any questions?"

Day 3: Convergence: Participants remain seated, writing materials—"Image Component" page and pencil—on desk and relaxing music in the background.

1. Say, "Do not speak until directed. Review the components in each column of your worksheet, especially the difference between the first column and the second." Pause.

2. "Now, as you softly breathe in and out through your nose ... breathing in ... and out ... in ... and out ... closing your eyes ... breathing easily, allowing my voice to guide you ... as all ... other sounds ... fall ... into the background—the sound of movement, of breathing, of thinking falling into the background."

3. "Focusing on the sound of my voice, becoming more relaxed, move your attention from the outside surface of your body to your relaxing muscles ... feeling yourself relaxing even more ... relaxed with every thought ... as you journey inward." Pause. "From here, you can remember your *limiting* sentence from day one ... taking time for all the visual components of this sentence to take shape into a picture." Pause. "Now place the picture over on the left side of your mind." Pause.

4. "Now, on the right side of your mind, recall yesterday's visual image for the decision labeled *No Difference* ... taking time for all the visual components of *No Difference* to take shape." Pause five seconds.

5. "Now get ready ... and quickly move both pictures to the middle of your mind—*No Difference* on top and all components changing to match *No Difference*. Long pause. "Looking through *No Difference* like magic to *limiting*, see both with the components

of *No Difference.*" Pause. "And now let them slide into the background ... and rest." Long pause.

6. "Coming back to this present moment, moving your attention to the outside surface of your body ... the pressure of your body against the seat and the air on your face ... feeling relaxed ... open your eyes, being fully present and ready to work." Pause. "You may speak to the group. Are there any questions or comments?"

Day 4: Enhancement: Participants remain seated, writing materials—"Component" page and pencil—on desk and relaxing music playing in the background.

1. Say, "Do not speak until directed. We will begin a magic journey. As you softly breathe in and out through your nose ... closing your eyes ... allowing my voice to guide you ... as all ... other sounds ... fall ... into the background ... becoming more relaxed with every thought ... as you journey inward ... deep inside where all truth resides ... you are able to find a place of peace and wisdom." Pause.

2. "In this place, you can find a different statement that, when listened to, moves you toward success, a statement such as "I can succeed at anything when I stick with it." Or one that, when you hear it, makes you feel bigger, more complete; the one that opens your resources to you; the one, when used, that makes your life more satisfying, more successful; the one that gives you confidence to spell or multiply correctly ... to make better grades or important choices, to speak up for yourself and follow your dream." Pause. "There are many times when this has been true, so now, as you listen, you believe what you hear to be true about yourself." Pause.

3. "Notice that when you put all these successful moments together ... you can easily complete the sentence "I am ...," or the sentence "I am more ...," or "I have all the ..." Pause. "Moreover, others tell you your sentence is true, and you agree. There is evidence to prove it." Pause.

4. Now, while in this place ... you can take time to notice the visual components of your positive statement." Pause. "Put it into a form you can see." Pause. "Is it moving or still?" Pause. "Is it in color or black and white?" Pause. "Is it close or far away?" Pause. "Are you looking at it or are you in it?" Long pause.

5. "Now bring this information back with you to this present moment ... moving your attention to the outside surface of your body ... the pressure of your body against the seat and the air on your face ... feeling relaxed ... Open your eyes, being fully present and ready to work." Pause.

6. "Write your positive statement on your worksheet and check the components of this *enhancing* statement in the day 4 column." Allow time to write.

7. "Compare the components of your *limiting* statement with those of your *enhancing* one. Draw a circle around the components in the day 4 column that are different from those in column one." Pause for writing. "You may speak to the group. Are there any questions?"

Day 5: Abundance: Participants remain seated. Begin with relaxing music playing in the background.

1. Say, "Do not speak until directed. We will begin by recalling the already discovered self-limiting information. As you softly breathe in and out through your nose ... breathing in ... and out ... in ... and out ... closing your eyes ... breathing easily, allowing my voice to guide you ... as all ... other sounds ... fall ... into the background, the sound of movement, of breathing, of thinking falling into the background."

2. "Focusing on the sound of my voice, becoming more relaxed ... moving your attention from the outside surface of your body ... to your relaxing muscles ... feeling yourself relaxing even more ... relaxing with every thought ... as you journey inward." Pause. "Deep inside where all truth resides, you are able to find a place of peace and wisdom, and you do."

3. "From here, you notice someone you admire ... someone who possesses the very thing you think is missing or limiting in yourself." Pause. "You become intrigued by how easily and completely this person moves and speaks ... from one activity to another ... how easy interactions with others are ... Long pause.

4. "To your surprise, this person notices your admiration and comes closer ... and offers to share these resources with you ... to help you have ... *completed success* too."

5. "When this person speaks, you hear the words "I have more than enough. You may have some of mine" ... and you accept the offered gift—an invitation to walk in the other person's shoes. You try it out." Pause. "You are surprised now at how easily ... *you do what you want to do.*" Pause. "You wonder, *How will my life be different?* And to your surprise, you find yourself alone in the back row of a movie theater and see the answer to your question unfold. The movie playing is from the future, and there you are on the screen, older." Pause. "You still have the gift of success you accepted long ago. You are impressed with what you see, and you hear yourself differently." Pause. "You decide to move closer to the screen for a better look ... From this perspective,

you see the future results of all your efforts … *change for the better* … before your eyes—relationships, grades, dreams, and skills improve!"

6. "You like what you see and decide to step up onto the stage and into your movie, walking into your body, becoming you, the star … feeling and moving easily with your new resources, knowing this is the real you." Pause.

7. "With this shift in perception, you recognize the lie in the limitations of the past. You place new affirming, *enhancing* words in these sentences: "I am …," or the sentence "I am more …, or "I have all the …" Pause. "You are pleased. You look around and quickly thank those who have helped you thus far." Pause.

8. "With new understanding … stepping out of the movie onto the stage, moving toward the doors of the theater, you walk out into the light of your new world." Pause. "You come back to this present moment, moving your attention to the outside surface of your body … the pressure of your body against the seat … the air on your face … feeling relaxed … Open your eyes, being fully present and ready to work." Pause. "You may speak to the group.""

Verification of Participants' Understanding: Review participants' journal entries or the completed "Image Component Comparison List" for understanding the component differences—*limiting* belief versus an *enhancing* one.

Reinforce with Independent Activity: Direct participants to recall self-enhancing statements before beginning something new and when taking tests.

MANAGING MY MIND

Nurture your mind with great thoughts, for you will never go any higher than you think.

—Benjamin Disraeli

We don't see things as they are. We see them as we are.

—Talmud

Lesson 13: Opportunities for Change

Grade Level: 6–12

Note: Teach this lesson in five separate sessions.

Purpose and Overview—Read Aloud:

We humans hold a magic wand—free will. It enables us to choose what we think and do. However, all too often, we create inertia with the erroneous belief that we cannot control our own thinking. We fall prey to mental clatter and confusion, drugs or alcohol. We forfeit our free will by giving away our own power. The following information was first presented in *Healing Mind, Five Steps to Ultimate Healing, Four Rooms for Thoughts: Achieve Satisfaction through a Well-Managed Mind* (Janice McDermott 2015).

Through free will, we are able to organize our minds to create our best potential. McDermott offers an easy way to organize the mind using the metaphor of a house with rooms that contain four distinct mental characteristics Each shape represents a different room of the mind. Our free will determines the sorting of thoughts into their designated category, which determines where and how each will influence our life. Then, using our free will, we choose which character in our mental house will manifest in our muscles, voice, and emotions, and we will be in control from moment to moment.

Note: Each of the four divisions has its own voice and its own body posture when we speak. Be sure to find them after each lesson and demonstrate to the group. Pair participants and have each individual demonstrate to their partner. Laughing indicates that you are not really putting your whole self into the role characteristics of each part.

Objective: Participants will be able to organize their thinking in a way that will provide emotional comfort and build self-esteem.

Present this lesson in five different sessions, one for each of the four rooms of the mind and one to unify the rooms.

Materials Needed for All Five Lessons:
1. Imagery script or Counselor Edition: Audio-Guided Imagery, Volume 2, track 10, "Mentor" (5:11); track 11, "Critic (5:59); track 12, "Nurturer" (7:24); track 13, "Child" (7:13), Volume 3, track 1, "My Mind" (6:40)
2. A display of weekly title and quote
3. Handouts from appendix: "The House of Mind," "Characteristics of Mental Rooms," "Observing My Mind Questionnaire," and "My House of Mind"
4. A pencil and the empty house copy of "My House of Mind" for each participant; same copy is used at each session

Session 1: Read Overview Aloud

The mentor (rectangle shape), modeled after the archetypical *Book of Life*, holds all personal beliefs as well as all the acquired information through living. The mentor is that part of you that is concerned with creating a more satisfying life. It wakes you up without an alarm clock; it tells you when you have passed your exit on the freeway while daydreaming. It is the part of you reading this page or hearing, taking in, and storing this information.

The mentor serves as an ally of your higher self, that power from which you seek guidance. It contains all of your values and beliefs, including those that are contradictory or filed *forgotten*. It is the keeper of all learned factual, none emotional data.

Imagine that every bit of information about yourself and you in the world is in a sequential timeline in front of you, beginning on your left, when you were born, and ending on your right, at your death. It is never erased or written over; only new events and information are added. Your belief in Santa at age four is still there, and your belief in Santa later as an archetypal figure is there as well. They are not in conflict. They mark time. They just are.

Your mentor supports your basic life purpose without judgments or emotions. This positive part of yourself makes only none emotional factual observations. The mentor does not receive or generate the emotional sting that taints critical statements. It recognizes dysfunction or poor form without a reaction to what it recognizes.

From the mentor state of mind, we see and have a choice to choose an action rather than an automatic knee-jerk response from the position of judging. This creates a clear space for a loving presence.

Mentor Characteristics:
1. Neutral body posture
2. Instructive
3. None emotional
4. Contains factual data
5. Contains accumulated beliefs and values even if contradictory
6. Knows the positive intent of dialogue in other rooms
7. Stores time, sequence of events, and other information as a computer would—think of a robot

Appendix Handouts:
1. "My House of Mind": have participants draw in their empty house a rectangular room for their mentor, leaving space for three more rooms
2. "Observing My Mind Questionnaire"

Read imagery script or listen to the Audio-Guided Imagery, Counselor Edition Volume 2, track 10, "Mentor" (5:11).

Imagery Script:

The Mentor

Day 1: Participants remain seated with relaxing music in the background.

1. Say, "Do not speak until directed. As you breathe in and out through your nose, closing your eyes, allow my voice to guide you … as all other sounds fall into the background. You know you have complete control over your imagination and are free to go wherever you like within your own mind. Becoming more relaxed … move your attention from the outside surface of your body, the air on your face,

your relaxing muscles." Pause. "Feeling more relaxed with every thought … you can journey inward." Pause.

2. "Imagine that you are standing in the center of a large circular room. As you look around, you see doors leading off in four opposing directions. Locate door one and notice its size and color. See the word *mentor* written on this door. This leads to a large rectangular room called MENTOR, the room of wisdom. There are no emotions in this room, only information. Open the door and walk in.

3. "In this room, you find all the information you have collected in your life. Take some time to look around, moving among the files, noticing the robotic sound of your voice reading facts off a page. You notice how neutral you feel speaking in this reading voice with no emotion."

4. "This room contains your accumulated beliefs and values, even contradictive. You can find the time you believed in Santa … and the time you saw behind the scenes of Santa … Time and sequence of events are stored here."

5. "In this mentor room, you can know about all the other rooms when you choose. All the information stored here is for constructive purposes only. There are no judgments, only facts." Pause. "This is the room to use when you want to appear poised, when interviewing for a job, or pleading your case without crying or losing your temper."

6. "The room called mentor has an expression in your body as well as your mind. Experience this in your body now." Pause. Listen once more to your robotic voice speaking your address. Notice the absence of emotions." Pause. "Now take one more look around before leaving this room and returning to the circular room." Pause.

7. "Come back to this present moment, moving your attention to the outside surface of your body … the pressure of your body against the seat … the air on your face … feeling relaxed."

8. "Keeping your eyes closed, quickly say aloud, along with everyone else in this room, your name and address three times without stopping. Begin now." Instructor says own name and address three times as well to encourage participants. Pause for everyone to finish."

9. "Open your eyes, being fully present and ready to work." Pause. "Please stand up and speak aloud as directed."

10. "Feeling your body, repeat again three times your name and address. Begin now." Instructor says own name and address three times as well. Pause for everyone to finish.

11. Allow time for group discussion of each person's experience.

Verification of Participants' Understanding: answers to the experienced day's handout questions, appendix "Observing My Mind Questionnaire."

Session 2: Critic Overview—Read Aloud:

Unlike the mentor, our critic (square symbol), for most of us, is our largest and most vocal mental room. The critic rejects, discounts, criticizes, judges, condemns, punishes, argues, and destroys. We mistakenly give it the position of power and authority within our minds, and it becomes a slave driver, inflicting internal psychological abuse and mental anguish.

It can be active when we are silent, when we are talking, and even when we are asleep. It impersonates any face and voice to which we are vulnerable. It is a master of self-deception— one moment being illustriously beautiful, while the next pitifully mangled and dejected. It is a cheat and a liar, a wolf in sheep's clothing. Even though it may say it intends well, it is unknowingly an ally of the dark and dangerous side of life.

The critic uses the language of *should, must, have to, ought to, supposed to, needed to, stupid, dumb,* and many, many other negative statements. It usually uses the voice of a critical parent or some other authority who wants to be in control by demanding *better.*

Keep in mind that this internal voice, even though it sounds familiar, is a product of your own making and not of society. It is a product of your development, and you are the one responsible for its continued influence in your life now. It is in *your* mind! However, it is someone else's rules and beliefs. When they are your values and beliefs, they say, "I want to," and "I intend to."

Critic Characteristics:
1. Tense body muscles
2. Incapable of love
3. Feels no guilt
4. Can appear suddenly
5. Attempts to gain recognition, remain important
6. Eavesdrops and interrupts other mental processes
7. Creates personal suffering, illusion of separateness, despair, and is destructive

The way our family interacted, nurtured, and disciplined is our family model of operations. It is the template for how our minds continue to work. In our minds, we treat ourselves the same way we were treated growing up. *What was missing then is still missing now—until we redesign our mental models to produce a sense of completeness in ourselves.*

Note: A participant abused by his internal critic will act shameful and guilty even in times of innocence.

Handout "My House of Mind" and "Observing My Mind Questionnaire"
1. Have participants draw a square room for their critic, leaving space for two more rooms
2. "Observing My Mind Questionnaire"

Read imagery script or play recording Audio-Guided Imagery Counselor Edition, Volume 2, track 11, "Critic" (5:59).

Imagery Script:

The Critic

Day 2: Participants remain seated with relaxing music playing in the background.

1. Say, "Do not speak until directed. As you breathe in and out through your nose, closing your eyes, allow my voice to guide you ... as all other sounds fall into the background. Becoming more relaxed ... move your attention from the outside surface of your body to the air on your face to your relaxing muscles." Pause. "Feeling more relaxed with every thought ... you journey inward." Pause.
2. "Imagine that you are standing in the center of your large circular room. You see the doors in four opposite directions. Locate door number one, with *mentor* written on the outside. Now, turning to your left, find door number two, labeled CRITIC. This leads to the square room with cracks in its walls for eavesdropping on the other rooms."
3. "The contents of this room are *destructive*. In this room, where love is impossible ... are all the faces and voices of the people who pop into your mind to cause you suffering with the illusion of separateness and despair ... the room of lots of *should, ought to,* and *guilt.* It is crowded in this room."
4. "Now, standing in front of door number two, you put on your insulated suit of armor and prepare to enter the room of the critic." Pause. "As you enter, notice the faces and voices coming from the dark corners." Pause. "You may recognize your own voice silently speaking or someone else's voice ... recorded in your mind long ago." Pause.
5. "Allow one voice to rise above all the others." Pause. "And from behind your armor, listen to the words ... Listen again to make sure you are hearing them correctly, and as you do, notice, even with your armor, how tense your body becomes." Pause. "Take a moment to observe where your tension begins when you listen to this voice." Pause.

"Where does your tension end?" Long pause. "Take one more look around before leaving ... Walk out, close the door, and stand in the circular room." Pause.

6. "In the circular room, take off your body armor, feel your body letting go of the tension of the critic, breathing easy, becoming lighter ... and more relaxed." Pause.

7. "Again, moving your attention to the outside surface of your body ... the air on your face and the pressure of your body against the seat, feeling relaxed ... open your eyes, being fully present and ready to work." Pause.

8. "Write the sentence you heard in the room of the critic. Note whether the voice saying it is (1) male or female, (2) mean or nice, (3) someone you know or not." Pause for writing. "Are there any questions or comments?"

Verification of Participants' Understanding: Answers to the experienced day's questions on handout "Observing My Mind Questionnaire."

Session 3: Nurturer Overview—Read Aloud:

The nurturer (heart symbol) characteristics are the ones used for many centuries to describe the personality of Jesus. These characteristics include being unconditionally loving, even to the critic, in addition to nonjudgmental, forgiving, intuitive, protective, constructive, accepting, creative, and purposeful. The nurturer unconditionally loves even the critic. The nurturer helps resolve the feelings involved with grief, such as anger, depression, hurt, remorse, sadness, and loneliness. The nurturer does this by listening to, acknowledging, and accepting the inner child's feelings. It treats our child part with respect and acceptance.

The nurturer gives specific to-the-point praise and is honest. It uses "I" messages rather than "you." Example: "I love you. I like you the way you are. I want you to be happy." The nurturer involves the creative inner child in problem-solving and decision-making relative to his or her own needs and is respectful toward the inner child's feelings, needs, wants, suggestions, and wisdom. A contented inner child means a happier adult. *Remember, heart energy never runs out, and we can send it through our thoughts.*

Nurturer Characteristics
1. Relaxed open-hearted body posture
2. Buffers the effects of the critic
3. Unconditionally loving (even to the critic)
4. Peaceful, forgiving
5. Nonjudgmental, accepting, validating

6. Intuitive, creative
7. Protective, constructive
8. Purposeful

Handouts:
1. "My House of Mind" and "Observing "My Mind Questionnaire."
2. Have participants draw in "My House of Mind" a heart-shaped room for their nurturer, leaving space for one more room.

Read imagery script or play Audio-Guided Imagery Counselor Edition, Volume 2, track 12, "Nurturer" (7:24).

Imagery Script:

The Nurturer

Day 3: Participants remain seated with relaxing music in the background.

1. Say, "Do not speak until directed. As you breathe in and out through your nose, closing your eyes, allow my voice to guide you … as all other sounds fall into the background. Becoming more relaxed … move your attention from the outside surface of your body, the air on your face, your relaxing muscles." Pause. "Feeling more relaxed with every thought … you journey inward." Pause.
2. "Imagine that you are once again standing in the center of your large circular room. You see the door labeled *mentor* and remember your body sense of being neutral, robotic." Pause. "You turn toward your left, see the door labeled critic, and remember the body sense of being tense." Pause. "You shudder and turn back to stand in front of the door of the mentor, regaining your solid, neutral, poised self." Pause.
3. "Breathing deeply, you look to your right at door number three. You can barely see the words written at the top. You move a little closer and are able to make out the word *nurturer.*"
4. "You observe light spilling out around the edges of the door and become curious. Gently placing your hand on the latch, you quietly open the door and look in. The light is so bright that you can only make out the heart shape of the room … and then the misty figure of a person with a familiar voice starts to take form, and familiar words you have longed to hear are spoken." Pause. "Whose voice is that?" Pause. "As you move closer, the voice changes to another pleasing voice of someone else speaking

more words you long to hear." Pause. "You pause to listen to the words again." Long pause.

5. "These words are like magic, causing you to feel loved and peaceful. You could stay here forever, for in this room there is unconditional love for all who enter. In here, there is no need for armor." Pause.

6. "You notice that you can feel peaceful … forgiving and accepting … validating … intuitive and creative … protective and purposeful, and all … the information from this room is constructive. You may hear other things such as You are wanted, You are beautiful, smart, clever … You are fun to be with … You are valued; you are hardworking." Pause.

7. Slowly say, "Now you can use these generous … loving and kind … pleasing … reassuring words to restructure your thoughts … to allow the activation and nurturing of your whole self, and you do." Pause one minute.

8. "Turning back toward the door … you linger a moment to hear those sweet words one more time." Pause one minute. "Walking out, you close the door behind you."

9. "Standing in the circular room, you notice that you are glowing and decide in the future to return to the room of the nurturer many more times." Pause.

10. "Again, moving your attention to the outside surface of your body … the air on your face and the pressure of your body against the seat, feeling relaxed … open your eyes, being fully present and ready to work." Pause.

11. "Write the words you heard in the room of the nurturer and note whether the voice saying it was male or female and if it was someone you know or do not know." Pause for writing. "Are there any questions or experiences to share?"

Verification of Participants' Understanding: Answers to the experienced day's questions on handout "Observing My Mind Questionnaire," found in the appendix.

Session 4: Inner Child Overview—Read Aloud:

The inner child (star symbol), sometimes called the divine child is the oldest part of our personality but appears to us as no older than six years of age. This core creative energy, identified as our inner child, is unique in each of us. Our inner child holds our full potential. To reach this compelling force, we must travel back from whence we came, back through the gateway of childhood, and hence become an even younger and younger child in order to reach the gateway to our universal energy—the opening between the spiritual and physical world whereby we embrace our total personalities both consciously and unconsciously, our true selves. It is accessed through meditation, a half-awake, half-asleep state of self-hypnosis.

It does not speak aloud but is heard internally by the nurturer and mentor. The mentor can report without emotion from its own body and voice what the child says.

Child Characteristics:
1. Relaxed, surrendering posture (usually nonvocal)
2. Ceaselessly creative
3. Finds a sense of value present in everything
4. Spontaneous
5. Source of all basic emotions
6. Eternally connected to the nonphysical

Note: Each of the four divisions has its own voice and its own body posture when we speak. However, *the child does not talk aloud, only internally.* It only communicates internally with the nurturer, and what it says or wants is spoken aloud by the listening neutral mentor.

Handouts:
1. Have participants draw a heart-shaped fourth room for their inner child in "My House of Mind."
2. Answer the questions in "Observing My Mind Questionnaire."

Read imagery script or play Audio-Guided Imagery, Counselor Edition Volume 2, track 13, "Child" (7:13).

Imagery Script:

The Child

Day 1: Participants remain seated with relaxing music in the background.

1. Say, "Do not speak until directed. As you breathe in and out through your nose, closing your eyes, allow my voice to guide you ... as all other sounds ... fall into the background. Becoming more relaxed, moving your attention from the outside surface of your body, the air on your face, to your relaxing muscles ... feeling more relaxed with every thought ... you can journey inward." Pause.
2. Imagine that you are once again standing in the center of your large circular room. You see the door labeled MENTOR and remember the body sense of being neutral, being none emotional, robotic." Pause. "Turning your attention toward your left, you see the door labeled critic and remember the body sense of being tense, and you tense more;

you shiver, shaking off the tension, turn back in the direction of the MENTOR door, and gain your composure." Pause.

3. "Looking to your right, you see the light spilling from the crack around the door called NURTURER, and you linger for a moment to enjoy again the body sensations that come from this heart-shaped room." Pause. "As you relax more, you notice the familiar glow again coming off your body." Pause.

4. "And now it is time to discover what is behind the fourth door. You may notice a tingle of excitement moving up your spine as you read the words printed in large letters: DOOR OF THE CHILD." Pause. "You gently open this door into a magical star-shaped room filled with children of all ages under six years old." Pause.

5. "You watch these children engaged in various activities, something all children need ... and you begin to notice other children present who, in addition to needing *love and stimulation*, also need *someone to listen*." Long pause. "You also see those children who need *positive attention ... validation ...* and *companionship*." Pause. "And another group needing *more information* and seeking a teacher." Pause. "And then there are those needing the *security of good boundaries*." Pause. "A few of the children need the *freedom to use their imaginations* without criticism." You see all of them ... and all of them ... see the glow emanating from you ... and begin to hope." Pause.

6. "An unusual thing starts to happen; one child steps out from all the rest ... and takes your hand. Immediately, you recognize what this child wants, and like magic, the glow emanating from you creates exactly what this child needs." Pause. "You explain that somehow the two of you are the same person—the older you coming from the future to take care of the younger you, who has waited all this time." Pause.

7. "In return, the child gives you a gift ... a gift of being ceaselessly creative in your presence ... helping you find a sense of value present in everything ... being more spontaneous, and by producing an emotion whenever needed." Long pause.

8. "Satisfied with what has transpired, the child returns to the others. You suddenly realize that all the children are *you* ... so you promise yourself that you will return in the future to give each one what it needs." Pause. "You walk out of the room, closing the door behind you, and find yourself once again in the circular room, feeling satisfied." Pause.

9. "Again, moving your attention to the outside surface of your body ... the air on your face and the pressure of your body against the seat, feeling relaxed ... open your eyes, being fully present and ready to work." Pause.

10. "In your "Observing My Mind" handout, circle one need of the child you encountered in the room of the child. Does your child need (1) stimulation, (2) someone to listen, (3)

positive attention, (4) validation, (5) companionship, (6) more information, (7) security, or (8) freedom to imagine [pause for writing]? Think of something you can do today to show the child part of yourself that you care. Are there any questions or anything you want to share?"

Verification of Participants' Understanding: Participants are able to answer the experienced day's handout questions from "Observing My Mind Questionnaire" and "My House of Mind."

Session 5: Handout (appendix): a printed copy for each participant of "My House of Mind," with prespecified rooms as pictured on previous page.

1. Have participants compare their drawing of "My House of Mind" with the model handout copy. What is the same? What is different?
2. Provide an opportunity for discussion before continuing.

Note: Participants remain seated with relaxing music playing in the background.

Read imagery script or play Audio-Guided Imagery, Volume 3, track 1, "My Mind" (6:40).

Imagery Script:

My Mind

1. Say, "Do not speak until directed. As you breathe in and out through your nose, closing your eyes, allow my voice to guide you … as all other sounds fall into the background." Long pause. "Become aware of any tension in your body. Allow these muscles to tighten and speak to you." Pause. "Notice the tone of the words that come to mind." Pause. "Is there an unspoken *should* in this thought?" Pause. "Release your tension as you say in a neutral voice to yourself, '*Stop*'—stopping this critical thought and becoming more relaxed, moving your attention inward and feeling more relaxed with every thought." Pause.
2. In this inward relaxed place, use your free will to allow a nurturing kind thought, in words you want to hear, spoken clearly by a loving voice to you." Pause. "Take a minute, all the time in the world, to hear these wanted words again … and again … and again." Pause one minute.
3. "Returning your attention now to the outside surface of your body … the air on your face and the pressure of your body against the seat, feeling relaxed … and cared for … open your eyes, being fully present and ready to work." Pause.

Verification of Participants' Understanding: Appendix handout *"Observing My Mind Questionnaire."* Complete any remaining unanswered questions.

Reinforce with Independent Activity: Use the metaphor of *four rooms of the mind* for writing exercises. Example: Using the characteristics of the critic (see overview), critique stories from the critic's point of view—make judgments. Do the same from the point of view of the mentor—none emotional professional writing, from the nurturer—encouraging and supporting someone, and from the child—first-person writing as a child.

Other Resources:

Davis, Bruce and Davis, Genny Wright. 1950. *The Magical Child Within You.* Berkeley: Celestial Arts.

McDermott, Janice M.Ed. MSW. *Healing Mind, Five Steps to Ultimate Healing, Four Rooms for Thoughts: Achieve Satisfaction through a well-Managed Mind.* 1663 Liberty Drive Bloomington, IN: Balboa press, A division of Hay House. 2015

Oaklander, Violet. 1978. *Windows to our Children.* Moab: Real People Press.

Additional Notes:

LESSONS 14–15
BUILDING SELF-ESTEEM

ACCEPTANCE AND PRAISE OF SELF AND OTHERS

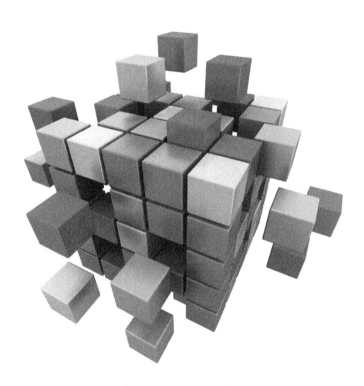

ACCEPTING MY SELVES

Friendship with oneself is all-important, because without it one cannot be friends with anyone else in the world.

—Eleanor Roosevelt

I looked and looked and this I came to see: That what I thought was you and you, Was really me and me.

–Ken Wilber

Lesson 14: Self-Esteem Building

Grade Level: 6–12-plus

Note: Lessons may be presented in three sessions, with the first two imagery activities in the first session.

Purpose and Overview: Deep inside every developing human being lies the erroneous belief that *others cannot see the parts of me that I have hidden away*. To survive in our families of origin, we learned to hide aspects of ourselves that failed to get approval. We created disapproval in our imaginations when we *interpreted* an event, or what someone said, or failed to say, as negative. Over time, our hidden aspects fall into our subconscious and are forgotten. We are left with a false belief that *something is wrong with me*. As years pass, we become more and more afraid of what we might discover if we look inside ourselves.

Dr. Carl G. Jung introduced the concept of a shadow self—unconscious, repressed, undeveloped, and denied parts of ourselves—and the law of opposites. According to Jung, "Everyone carries a shadow, and the less it is embodied in the individual's conscious life, the blacker and denser it is. At all counts, it forms an unconscious snag, thwarting our most well-meant intentions." Jung believed that no matter what we identify with in our personalities, whether desired or desirable, the opposite is present in our unconsciousness. We discover these hidden parts of ourselves by using other people as our mirrors, saying in response to what we see, "And so am I." In this way, we accept *all* as *me*—taking total responsibility for our lives rather than blaming others and feeling less than we are.

Accepting responsibility changes the outcome of our lives. What goes on inside is reflected on the outside from day to day. As Ken Weber said, "I looked and looked and this I came to see: That what I thought was you and you, Was really me and me." Our destinies are of our own making.

Everyone shares all human characteristics. Like the Rubik's Cube toy, each of us is trying to get one favorite color out front. We can be a thief when we are starving, a murderer when in war. All the characteristics observed in another are also characteristics of the observer. If we say someone is so fun, then we must say, "And so am I." Try it. Own your shadow.

Psychotherapists claim that *if you can see it, you have it, both the desired and the undesirable.* All human characteristics are wells of strengths and talents untapped, waiting to fuel the realization of our dreams. In our imaginations, we can *dance* in a safe way with the shadow aspects of ourselves while playing with various outcomes, growing more comfortable and accepting of ourselves. Our goal over time is to be free in our imaginations, to face ourselves with courage. The more we know about ourselves, the more choices we have.

A brain-integrating activity such as guided imagery helps us accept our hidden selves, reclaiming our power and creativity while raising our self-esteem.

Objective: Participants will be able to explore opposites as a way of enhancing and developing self-acceptance.

Materials Needed:
1. Imagery script or Grand Ideas from Within Counselor Edition: Audio-Guided Imagery, Volume 3, track 2,
    "Shadow Dancing A" (6:31); track 3, "Shadow Dancing B" (6:10); track 4, "My Animal" (7:05); track 5, "Admiration" (6:30)
2. Paper and pencil
3. A display of weekly title, quotes

Present Lesson Overview (and read or play imagery activities):
Day 1: Participants remain seated with relaxing music playing in the background.

1. Say, "Do not speak until directed. As you breathe in and out through your nose … closing your eyes, allow my voice to guide you … as all … other … sounds fall into the background, and you know you have complete control over your imagination and are free to go wherever you like within your own mind. Becoming more relaxed … move your attention from the outside surface of your body … to the air on your face to your relaxing muscles. Feeling more relaxed with every thought, allowing yourself to journey inward." Pause.

2. "Imagine that you are walking down a long sunny path … Just ahead of you is a line that separates light from dark, and at that line is a gate, and on that gate is a sign that reads SHADOW WORLD. Feeling brave, you open the gate and step into the world of semi light and shadows, another world of streets, buildings, and gray shadows, people coming and going. Everyone is the opposite of you, for you are from the world of light."

3. "At first, you want to see their faces and the color of their hair and eyes, but you find it is only your imagination and that all that really exists are shadows."

4. "You decide to introduce yourself and get to know someone. You soon discover that there are different rules for friendship in the shadow world. In this world, you must dance with each other before you can talk. You must choose your best quality to present to your shadow choice, who is automatically your opposite. You think about choosing your "I am nice self" and decide that you are not ready to meet your shadow, "I am mean." So you choose your next best characteristic and prepare to meet the opposite." Pause.

5. "Your opposite moves toward you and bows. You bow in return and begin to move in unison with each other." Pause. "You dance and move, creating new steps and routines, new places to go, and things to do." Long pause.

6. "As you pass by the light from the gate, you see the shadow becoming clearer. You see your face looking back at you. Confused, you ponder how this could be … and yes, you can accept the fact that you are able to bring *you* out of the shadows and into the real world … and so … you allow your shadow opposite to attach to your body and walk out with you into the light, accepting the responsibility of being one way sometimes and the opposite at others." Pause. "Walking back up the path, returning to a state of presence, moving your attention to the outside surface of your body … the air on your face and the pressure of your body against the seat, feeling relaxed and alert … open your eyes, being fully present and ready to work." Pause.

7. "Take thirty seconds to write a description of you as your chosen characteristic and you as your shadow characteristic." Pause thirty seconds. "Is there anything you would like to share?"

Day 2: Participants remain seated with relaxing music playing in the background.

1. Say, "Do not speak until directed. As you breathe in and out through your nose ... closing your eyes, allow my voice to guide you ... as all ... other ... sounds fall into the background. Becoming more relaxed ... move your attention from the outside surface of your body ... to the air on your face, to your relaxing muscles. Feeling more relaxed with every thought, allow yourself to journey inward." Pause.
2. "Imagine that you are walking down a long sunny familiar path ... and just ahead of you is the familiar gate between light and dark with the sign that reads SHADOW WORLD. Knowing what to expect, you open the gate and step into the world of semi light and shadows, the other world of streets, buildings, and shadow people coming and going. Everyone is the opposite of you."
3. "It takes a moment for your eyes to adjust to the idea that you see only shadows. Remembering there are different rules for friendship in the shadow world and that in this world you must dance with the other before you can speak."
4. "You choose your worst quality this time to present to your shadow opposite, who is your best quality." Pause. "You begin to bend and move in your worst way, without grace or form, like a beast of some kind." Pause. "Out of the shadow with grace and ease steps the opposite form of you. Your opposite moves toward you and bows. You bow in return and begin to move in unison—one moving in awkwardness and the other in grace." Pause. Increase voice Volume and tempo to build intensity. "You dance and move, creating new steps and routines, new places to go and things to do." Long pause.
5. Say slower, "As you pass by the light from the door, you see the shadow becoming clear. You looks back. You ponder again *how this could be* ... and yes, you can accept the fact that you are able to bring *you* out of the shadows and into the real world." Pause. "Accepting the responsibility of being one way sometimes and the opposite at others, you allow another one of your shadow opposites to attach to your body and walk out with you into the light. You notice that you can feel fuller and more confident." Pause.
6. "You walk back up the path ... returning to a state of presence, moving your attention to the outside surface of your body ... the air on your face and the pressure of your

body against the seat, feeling relaxed and alert ... Open your eyes, being fully present and ready to work." Pause.

7. "Take thirty seconds to write a description of you as your chosen characteristic and you as your shadow characteristic." Pause one minute. "Put your materials away. Is there anything you would like to share?"

Day 3: Participants remain seated with relaxing music playing in the background.

1. "Say, "Do not speak until directed. As you breathe in and out through your nose ... closing your eyes, allow my voice to guide you ... as all ... other ... sounds fall into the background. Becoming more relaxed ... moving your attention from the outside surface of your body ... to the air on your face, to your relaxing muscles ... feeling more relaxed with every thought, allowing yourself to journey inward." Pause.

2. "Imagine that you step into a larger transparent colored balloon or ball. There is plenty of room for you to stand and walk around. You can move freely, and the balloon moves with you. It will not burst. It only stretches and expands as you freely move and walk. You begin to try it out, playfully walking through a park ... and just ahead of you, someone else is walking in a balloon of a different color. You move closer and notice it is someone you know, someone you admire and respect, and secretly wish you could be like that person." Pause.

3. "You say hello to each other and decide to walk together, each in your own balloon. You hear a funny sound and soon discover that your balloons are rubbing together. You laugh about it and decide to play a game." Pause.

4. "You both know how to use your minds to push your balloon into the other to create a middle section made of both colors of your balloons, and you watch the new color form between you." Pause. "You admire this new color, and both of you, at the same time, stick your arms into it, feeling what this new color feels like." Pause. "Wow! There is a different temperature and pleasing sensation." Pause. "Joining hands, the two of you step together into the new space as it expands to create lots of room ... and your own color expands along with it. You play and move in all directions in this new color, noticing the sounds ... smells ... the taste of the air and the view of the park through this blended shade of color." Pause. "You say your goodbyes and agree to meet again."

5. "You step back into your own balloon, returning to your own color as you notice that through this experience, your balloon has changed for the better, but you are not quite sure how. Is it stronger, rounder, bouncier, bigger, brighter, lighter, or ...? Whatever it is, with which you are pleased." Pause.

6. "Walking out of the park and now back to a state of presence, moving your attention to the outside surface of your body ... the air on your face and the pressure of your body against the seat, feeling relaxed and alert ... open your eyes, being fully present and ready to work." Pause.

7. "Using your five senses, take one minute to write a description of both your balloon and the mixed balloon." Pause one minute. "Put your journals away. Is there anything you would like to share?"

Day 4: Participants remain seated with relaxing music playing in the background.

1. Say, "Do not speak until directed. As you breathe in and out through your nose ... closing your eyes, allow my voice to guide you ... as all ... other ... sounds fall into the background. Becoming more relaxed, moving your attention from the outside surface of your body, the air on your face to your relaxing muscles." Pause. "Feeling more relaxed with every thought ... allow yourself to journey inward." Pause. "Imagine that you are walking down a long set of stairs that bring you deeper and deeper into yourself." Pause.

2. "There is a dim light in this space. You turn and look around. The edges are dark. In the far corner, you can barely make out the bars of a large cage. You decide to get a flashlight and take a closer look. With caution, you move toward it ... and as you do, you hear a crying sound." Pause. "There, crouched in the corner of the cage, is an animal. Shining your light on it, you are able to make out a form." Pause. "It looks well cared for, and you wonder if maybe you were the one who left it there in the care of someone else. You move closer, and as you do, the animal's eyes catch your eyes and you both stare deep into the other." Pause. "Without words, you communicate between you everything you need to know ... and the animal, trusting you, moves closer, reaching through the bars to touch you." Pause. "You reach back, moved by the gentleness you share."

3. "Other characteristics about this animal intrigue you. You make a mental note of each one." Pause. "Your animal offers these intriguing things to you as a gift. You accept and decide to unlock the cage, telling the animal it can come out whenever it likes because the two of you can live in harmony." Pause for thirty seconds.

4. "You turn, walk out of the room, and as you walk up the stairs you think you can remember someone saying the words, '*Self-image sets the boundaries of individual accomplishment*', and you ponder them, '*Self-image sets the boundaries of individual*

accomplishment'" (Maxwell Maltz, twentieth-century American psychologist and motivational writer).

5. "Returning to a state of presence … move your attention to the outside surface of your body … the air on your face and the pressure of your body against the seat, feeling relaxed … Open your eyes, being fully present and ready to work." Pause.

6. "Take one minute to draw an outline picture of your animal and to make a list of words that describe your animal." Pause one minute. "Is there anything you would like to share?"

Day 5: Participants are assigned a designated partner. All remain seated with relaxing music playing in the background.

1. Say, "Do not speak until directed. As you breathe in and out through your nose … closing your eyes, allow my voice to guide you … as all … other … sounds fall into the background. Becoming more relaxed … move your attention from the outside surface of your body, to the air on your face, to your relaxing muscles." Pause. "Feeling more relaxed with every thought … allow yourself to journey inward." Long pause.

2. "Imagine that you are walking down a long set of stairs that bring you deeper and deeper into yourself. In this place, sitting there in front of you is your total self with all the traits that exist, those you currently admire and those you do not, those you think you have and those you think you do not … *You* are … capable of anything."

3. "For some reason at this very moment, you hear someone say, 'A man cannot be comfortable without his own approval.' Those words *of* Samuel Clemens, known as Mark Twain, echo in your mind: '*A man cannot be comfortable without his own approval.*'" Pause.

4. You look again at your total self sitting peacefully in front of you and decide you can approve of all that you see. Walking over, turning, and sitting down into yourself, blending your form with your total self … you can feel what this is like … the sensations … the points of view … the choices … the new ideas … all emanating from you, through you, to you." Pause. "Enjoy being you." Pause one minute.

5. "Now you rise up." Pause. "Standing still for a moment to gain your balance … and walking back to the stairs to begin the climb back up to the external world … returning to a state of presence." Long pause.

6. "Moving your attention to the outside surface of your body … the air on your face and the pressure of your body against the seat … feeling relaxed … open your eyes, being fully present and ready to work." Pause.

7. "Turn to your designated partner and take fifteen seconds each to share your experiences. You may speak to your partner." Pause thirty seconds. "You may speak to the class. Are there any questions?"

Verification of Participants' Understanding: Group discussion or participants' written information showing an understanding of the positive potential in their opposite or unaccepted traits.

Reinforce with Independent Activity: Draw shapes to represent emerging aspects of the self or express them through color, movement, or by creating a drama. Choose one new positive behavior and begin using it at home or on the weekends.

Other Resources:
Wilber, Ken. 2000. *Integral Psychology*, Boston: Shambala Publications.

Additional Notes:

PRAISING SELF AND OTHERS

> To withhold deserved praise lest it should make its object conceited
> is as dishonest as to withhold payment of a just debt lest your creditor
> should spend the money badly.
>
> —George Bernard Shaw

Lesson 15: Internalizing Compliments

Grade Level: 6–12

Purpose and Overview: Through guided imagery, we can recall times when we learned something easily or quickly, memories of our positive aspects, and memories of others taking positive notice of us. These pleasant memories can help us encourage and motivate ourselves—especially in the room of the child (see lesson 13, day 5).

What we think about our memories determines how they affect us in the present. All too often, we fail to utilize these personal treasures. We discount pleasing recalled events, denying our experience as a once-in-a-lifetime event, a fluke, or an accident.

When someone offers us a bit of praise, we tend to devalue it with thoughts like, *They don't really know me* or *They don't know what they're talking about.* We fail to remember times of praise because they are rare, when in reality, this would be a reason to recall each instance.

Deflecting compliments is common in our competitive society. Not only do we deflect by what we think about compliments, but we also physically deflect by the way we initially receive them. We look away, avoiding direct eye contact with the person complimenting. We pretend they are talking to someone else. We may even catch the compliment and toss it back with a shrug or a roll of the eyes. We can ask for another piece of cake when we want more, but seldom do we ask someone to give us another compliment or to repeat a compliment so we can really enjoy it. We avoid complimenting ourselves for fear of sounding boastful. We keep up our guard, fearing some compliments are contaminated.

In fact, some compliments *are* contaminated—a *warm fuzzy* with a tacked on *cold prickle*. Contaminated compliments sound like this: *You did really well on that exam; too bad you can't do that all the time.* In these instances, we open our minds and bodies to receive the warm praise, only to have a negative tag follow. After contact with a few prickles, we become gun-shy, slow to open when a truly good warm fuzzy is present. We ask ourselves, *Can I trust this?*

Receiving praise is a circular process. Giving and receiving go together. What kind of praise giver are you? Do you contaminate your offer or think praise but withhold it?

Bill Clinton, the forty-second president of the United States, claims to have risen to success on the shoulders of his friends. Successful people are skilled in helping others recognize their finer qualities through praise, and Bill Clinton is very skilled. When we give honest praise to others, *they* become loyal to us, and *we* become successful.

Chris Widener, a popular speaker and writer, is also the president of Made for Success and Extraordinary Leaders, two companies that help individuals and organizations turn their potential into performance. Widener says, "Unlike candy, tokens, or money, social rewards are always available and help build strong positive relationships."

There is no better social reward than praise. When praising someone, stand close enough to look him or her in the eyes and smile. Touch the other person when appropriate and put emotion into your voice. Make your praise direct and specific. Rather than saying, "You are a hard worker" when a participant has completed a project, say, "I really like how you pay attention to detail. Your lettering is very neat." In addition, praise needs to occur during or soon after the behavior you are praising. The word *really* seems to be an important component of praising, when left out, the listener will not feel as satisfied.

A study of over twelve hundred samples shows how Americans use compliments (Manes and Wolfson 1980). The first three simple forms make up over 85 percent of the compliments given in English. The last three simple forms account for most of what is remaining. The word "really" seems to make the compliment more meaningful.

Compliment Percentage Structure:
1. Your dog is really cute (50 percent).
   Your (noun) is/looks really (adjective).
2. I really like your car (16.1 percent).
   I really like/love (noun).

3. That's a really interesting picture (14.9 percent).
   That's a really (adjective) (noun).
4. You did a really good job (3.3 percent).
   You (verb) a really (adjective) (noun).
5. You really handled that situation well (2.7 percent).
   You really (verb) (noun phrase) (adjective).
6. Nice game (1.6 percent).
   (adjective) (noun)

"People aspire to higher standards of performance when given genuine appreciation for their dedication and publicly recognized for their extraordinary achievements" *Encouraging the Heart: A Leader's Guide to Rewarding and Recognizing Others* (Kouzes and Posner).

"To whom much is given, much is required" (Luke 12:48 KJV). When we learn to fill our whole beings with an abundance of praise and compliments to the point of complete satisfaction, we can truly give to others from our abundance—creating and sustaining the circle of emotional nurturing and caring that is necessary for good mental health.

The following is a helpful reference for responding positively *to other people's emotions.* (Remember, *confusion* is a *thought,* not an emotion.)

4 Basic Emotions	Appropriate Responses
Glad	Join and participate
Mad	Respect and detach
Sad	Allow and support
Afraid	Reassure and protect

Objective: Participants will be able to use praise to build self-esteem and personal relationships.

Materials Needed:
1. Imagery script and "Background Music," Grand Ideas from within Counselor Edition, Volume 3, track 9
2. Grand Ideas from within Counselor Edition, Audio-Guided Imagery, Volume 3, track 6 Praising Self (6:20), track 7 Praising Others (5:02), track 8 Praise Practice (4:31)
3. Pencil and paper for each participant, display of lesson title, quote, and the additional quote "To whom much is given much is required" (Luke 12:48 KJV).

Present Lesson Overview:
Read guided imagery script while playing Volume 3, track 9, "Background Music," or while playing imagery audio, Volume 3, tracks 6–8.

Imagery Script:

Praising Self
Audio Volume 3, track 6

Days 1–2: Participants remain seated with relaxing music playing in the background.

1.   Say, "Do not speak until directed. As you breathe in and out through your nose, closing your eyes, allow my voice to guide you … as all other sounds fall into the background, and you know you have complete control over your imagination and are free to go wherever you like within your own mind. Becoming more relaxed, move your attention from the outside surface of your body to the air on your face and your relaxing muscles." Pause. "Feeling more relaxed with every thought … you journey inward." Pause.

2.   "In this inward space, you can recall times when you learned something easily or quickly … memories of your positive aspects, as well as memories of others noticing you in a positive way." Pause. "You can use these memories now to encourage and motivate yourself—all those children in the room of the child." Pause.

3.   "Find a time, a memory, when someone told you something about yourself in a praising manner." Long pause. "Hear these praising words again. Notice the Volume … rhythm … one … and emotion in the voice." Pause. "Observe the facial expressions of the speaker and notice how you feel." Long pause.

4.   "Find another time or memory when someone told you something about yourself in a praising manner." Long pause. "Hear these praising words again. Notice the Volume … rhythm … tone … and emotion in the voice. Observe their facial expressions and how you feel." Pause.

5.   "Take these positive intended words to the door of the child; open the door and wait a moment for a child to approach you … As you touch and smile, say these positive words to the child." Pause. "Notice your Volume, rhythm, tone, and emotion in your voice. Feel the expression on your face. Repeat your statement so the child can hear the words again and enjoy them." Long pause. "When you are ready, turn and leave this room, closing the door behind you."

6. "Returning to a state of presence, moving your attention to the outside surface of your body … the air on your face and the pressure of your body against the seat, feeling relaxed and alert … Open your eyes, being fully present and ready to work." Pause.

7. "Take thirty seconds to write your praise sentences. Pause thirty seconds. "Look around the room. Is there someone to whom you can honestly give the same praise? If so, decide to speak one of your praise sentences to this person before the end of the week. Would you like to share your praise sentence? Are there any questions or comments?"

Imagery Script:

Praising Others
Audio Volume 3, track 7

Days 3–4: Participants remain seated with relaxing music playing in the background.

1. Say, "Do not speak until directed. As you breathe in and out through your nose, closing your eyes, allow my voice to guide you … as all other sounds fall into the background. Becoming more relaxed, moving your attention from the outside surface of your body to the air on your face and your relaxing muscles. Feeling more relaxed with every thought … you journey inward." Pause.

2. "In this inward space, recall times when you were encouraged and motivated by someone's words of praise or a memory when someone did something for you in a positive manner." Long pause. "You can use these memories as a model in the future to encourage and motivate others."

3. "Hear these praising words again. Notice the Volume … rhythm … tone … and emotion in the voices." Pause. "Observe the facial expressions and notice how you feel." Long pause.

4. "Now imagine you are walking toward someone your age who has a trait or skill you admire." Pause. "Feel your face as you smile, moving closer as you begin to speak praising words that are pleasing to hear." Pause. "Notice the person's response, which tells you if you are successful in delivering your praise." Pause. "Repeat your words of praise so this person can enjoy hearing them again." Long pause.

5. "When you are ready, say farewell, turn, and leave … returning to a state of presence, moving your attention to the outside surface of your body … the air on your face and the pressure of your body against the seat, feeling relaxed and alert … Open your eyes, being fully present and ready to work." Pause.

6. "Take thirty seconds to write your praise sentences and the name of the person receiving it in your journal." Pause thirty seconds. "Put your journals away. You may speak to the group."

Imagery Script:

Praise Practice
Audio, Volume 3, track 8

Day 5: Participants remain seated with relaxing music playing in the background and designated partner nearby.

1. Say, "Do not speak until directed. As you breathe in and out through your nose, closing your eyes, allow my voice to guide you ... as all other sounds fall into the background. Becoming more relaxed, moving your attention from the outside surface of your body to the air on your face and your relaxing muscles. Feeling more relaxed with every thought ... you journey inward." Pause.

2. "In this inward space, recall three traits about yourself that are praiseworthy." Long pause. "Now, finding the right Volume ... rhythm ... tone ... emotion ... and words for each of your praiseworthy traits ... hear yourself deliver them to the listening part of you." Pause. "Feel them find a home somewhere in your body." Long pause.

3. "Finishing ... begin to return to a state of presence, moving your attention to the outside surface of your body ... the air on your face and the pressure of your body against the seat, feeling relaxed and alert ... Open your eyes, being fully present and ready to work." Pause.

4. "Decide what you want to compliment about your designated partner and how to say it. Practice in your mind." Long pause. "The person receiving the compliment maintains direct eye contact and gives the appropriate response—a simple, sincere *thank-you*. You may speak to your partner to deliver these compliments." One-minute pause.

Verification of Participants' Understanding: Self-praising written statements and a willingness to receive praise and to recognize and praise positive attributes in others

Reinforce with Independent Activity: Encourage participants to do the following:

- Is there someone you know who is joyful, helpful, or honest? (Remember, if you can see a trait or characteristic, you have it.) Then let that other person know how much you appreciate that trait in him or her. You can do it with a word, a card, or a phone call. Look for and honestly praise positive character traits and actions of others around you. Make it your goal to praise at least five people a day.

- Use the kinds of compliments mentioned in the overview (Manes and Wolfson) to teach parts of speech. Have participants write their own example of each of the six kinds and read them to a partner to determine which form the partner prefers.

Other Resources:

Kouzes, James M. 2003. Posner, Barry Z., Posner, Barry Z. 2003. *Encouraging the* Heart: *A Leader's Guide to Rewarding and Recognizing Others.* Somerset: Jossey-Bass.

Wolfson, N., Manes, J. 1980 "The Compliment as a Social Strategy." Papers in Linguistics: International Journal of Human Communication 13, 3: 391–410.

Dakin S, A. J. Arrowood.1981 "The Social Comparison of Ability". Human Relations 34: 89–109.

Additional Notes:

LESSONS 16–18
SELF-ACTUALIZING

BECOMING ALL OF WHAT ONE IS
CAPABLE OF BECOMING

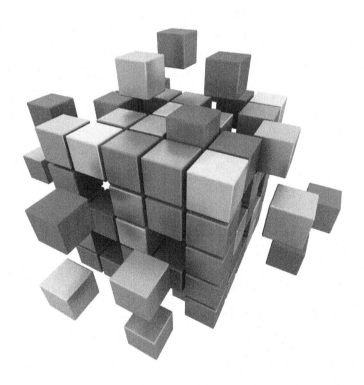

WINDS OF CHANGE

You are never given a wish without also being given the power to make it true. You may have to work for it, however.

—Richard Bach

Lesson 16: Directing Life's Changes

Grade Level: 6–12

Note: Present this lesson in two to three sessions. Complete *Change Process* steps 1–2 in the first session, using *Change Needs* imagery.

Purpose and Overview: Many of us go through our lives in a state of "comfortable discomfort," getting through each day but not enjoying life. Participants often feel they have no control over the events in their lives because school and family structure consume so much of their lives. As a result, participants may become hopeless about their ability to change anything or may blame others for their lot in life. Much energy is spent resisting or reacting to changes over which *we think* we have no control rather than using our energy to initiate small changes that can make a difference in our quality of life.

The Change Process (process of changing) involves
1. taking an objective look at life as it is now;
2. taking an objective look at current behaviors that contribute to discontent;
3. imagining new behavioral changes that would result in a more fulfilling life;
4. imagining how life would be different when the changes take hold; and
5. implementing the changes.

These exercises show participants a way to take responsibility for self-direction and positive changes in their lives.

Objective: Participants will be able to explore areas of their lives in need of change and then imagine the desired changes in order to create the desired results.

Materials Needed:

1. Imagery script with Volume 3, track 9, "Background Music," or play audio Grand Ideas from Within Counselor Edition, guided imagery Volume4, track 1, "Change Needs" (7:10); track 2, "Change Happens" (8:02); track 3, "Change Results" (7:20)

2. Display of weekly title and quote

3. Participant journal, writing and drawing tools

Present Lesson Overview: Read guided imagery script with Volume 4, track 9, "Background Music," or play imagery audio activities, Volume 4, tracks 1–3

Imagery Script:

Winds of Change

Day 1: Participants remain seated with relaxing music playing in the background.

1. Say, "Do not speak until directed. As you breathe in and out through your nose [pause], closing your eyes, allow my voice to guide you … as all … other … sounds fall into the background. You know you have complete control over your imagination and are free to go wherever you like within your own mind. Becoming more relaxed … move your attention from the outside surface of your body … and the air on your face … to your relaxing muscles." Pause. "Feeling more relaxed with every thought … allow yourself to journey inward." Pause.

2. "Imagine that you are walking down a path … experiencing the sights … sounds … feelings … and smells … all around you." Pause. "Enjoying the walk, you begin to notice your body filling with a sense of excitement. As you look ahead, you notice that the path leads to a large walled city. The wall is so tall that you cannot see over it, and your eyes, drawn to an immense gate, reveal an entrance to what lies behind the wall … You feel eager to explore what you cannot see … You do not know how to open the gate … or how to get a view of the other side."

3. "As you draw closer, you notice perched atop the gate a large magnificent eagle … watching you. You feel no fear … only curiosity. You wish that, just for a moment, you could become the eagle … and fly over the wall … see what is on the other side. Just as you have the thought, the eagle swoops toward you … and knowing that you are safe, the two of you become one … just for a little while. As you do, you feel the power of your wings as you soar through the air … feeling the wind … absorbing the sights and sounds around you … You then focus your attention on what lies beneath you … You are surprised to see your school, your home, and your neighborhood. You have a rare

opportunity to see your life through the eyes of the eagle … without fear … without judgment, so you soar closer and begin to see yourself … in your life as it is today."

4. Noticing yourself … in your life … behaving in ways that are harmful to you … in ways that you would like to change." Pause.

5. "Take a moment, which is all the time you need, to observe you … living your life as you do now—with family … with friends … with authority figures … at home … at school … wherever you may be." Pause.

6. "Having taken a safe, honest look at your life … you return to the ground … just outside the gate. Thanking the eagle for the clear vision … you walk back up the path … moving your attention to the outside surface of your body … the air on your face and the pressure of your body against the seat, feeling relaxed and alert." Pause. "Open your eyes, being fully present and ready to work." Pause.

7. "Take one minute to write or draw about one of your harmful behaviors, including how you feel being harmful." Pause one minute. "You may share with the group."

Imagery Script:

Change Needs
Volume 4, track 1

Day 2: Participants remain seated with relaxing music playing in the background.

1. Say, "As you breathe in and out through your nose … closing your eyes, allow my voice to guide you … as all … other … sounds fall into the background. Becoming more relaxed … move your attention from the outside surface of your body … and the air on your face … to your relaxing muscles." Pause. "Feeling more relaxed with every thought … allow yourself to journey inward." Pause.

2. "Imagine that you are walking down a path … experiencing the sights … sounds … feelings … and smells … all around you." Pause. "Enjoying the walk, you begin to notice your body filling with a sense of excitement. As you look ahead, you notice that you are on the path leading to the large walled city. The wall is so tall that you cannot see over it, and your eyes, drawn to an immense gate, reveal an entrance to what lies behind the wall. Once again, you feel eager to explore what you cannot see.

3. "As you draw closer, you notice perched atop the gate that large magnificent eagle … watching you. You feel no fear … only curiosity, and in a moment, you and the eagle agree to become one … and as you do, you begin to fly over the wall … seeing what is on the other side, absorbing the sights and sounds around you … You then focus your attention on what lies beneath you. You are surprised to see your school, your

home, and your neighborhood." Pause. "You use this rare opportunity to see your life through the eyes of the eagle ... without fear ... without judgment. And so you soar closer and begin to see yourself ... in your life as it is today."

4. "Noticing yourself in your life ... behaving in ways that are harmful to you ... in ways that you would like to change." Pause. "Take a moment, which is all the time you need, to observe you ... living your life as you do now, with family ... with friends ... with authority figures at home, at school, at work ... wherever you may be behaving in a harmful way." Long pause.

5. "Having taken a safe, honest look at your life ... you return to the ground ... just outside the gate. Thanking the eagle for your clear vision ... you walk back up the path ... moving your attention to the outside surface of your body ... the air on your face and the pressure of your body against the seat, feeling relaxed and alert ... Open your eyes, being fully present and ready to work." Pause. "Take one minute to write or draw about another one of your harmful behaviors, including how you feel being harmful in this way." Pause one minute. "You may speak to the group."

Day 3: Participants remain seated with relaxing music playing in the background.

Imagery Script:

Change Happens
Volume 3, track 2

1. Say, "Do not speak until directed. As you breathe in and out through your nose ... closing your eyes, allow my voice to guide you ... as all ... other ... sounds fall into the background. Becoming more relaxed ... moving your attention from the outside surface of your body ... and the air on your face ... to your relaxing muscles ... feeling more relaxed with every thought ... allowing yourself to journey inward." Pause.

2. "Imagine that you are walking down a path ... experiencing the sights ... sounds ... feelings ... and smells ... all around you." Pause. "Enjoying the walk, you begin to notice your body filling with a sense of excitement. As you look ahead, you notice that you are on the path leading to the large walled city. The wall is so tall that you cannot see over it. As before, your eyes are drawn to the immense gate ... an entrance to what lies beyond the wall. You feel eager to explore again what you cannot see." Pause. "As you draw closer, you notice that the eagle is once again perched atop the gate that is impossible to open ... You feel no fear ... only curiosity; you think the thought that makes you and the eagle one, and again becoming one with the eagle flying over the wall ... to explore what is on the other side."

3. "Knowing that you are safe, the two of you feel the power of your wings as you soar through the air, no longer surprised to see your home, and your neighborhood, and your school. Once again, you have a rare opportunity to see your life through new eyes ... without fear ... without judgment, so you soar closer and begin to see yourself ... in your life as it is today, begin to melt, and reform into the way you'd like it to be ... new shapes, new sounds, new sensations, new feelings, new smells and tastes. Gliding on the winds of change, you fly through your changing life. You see yourself ... in your life ... behaving in ways that are helpful to you and to others ..." Now read slowly. "Making the changes you imagine in your life ... take a moment, which is all the time you need, to observe yourself ... living this life as you want ... with family ... with friends ... with authority figures ... at home ... at school ... wherever you may be." Pause one minute.

4. "Having taken a safe, honest look at the positive changes you can make in your life ... you return to the ground ... just outside the gate. Thanking the eagle for this clear vision ... you walk back up the path, moving your attention to the outside surface of your body ... the air on your face and the pressure of your body against the seat, feeling relaxed and alert ... Open your eyes, being fully present and ready to work." Pause.

5. "Take one minute to write or draw about one helpful change you see yourself making, including how you feel about making this change." Pause one minute. "Put your journals away. You may speak to the group."

Days IV–V: Participants remain seated with "Background Music" playing.

Imagery Script:

Change Results
Volume 3, track 3

1. Say, "Do not speak until directed. As you breathe in and out through your nose [pause], closing your eyes, allow my voice to guide you ... as all ... other ... sounds ... fall into the background. Becoming more relaxed ... moving your attention from the outside surface of your body ... and the air on your face ... to your relaxing muscles ... feeling more relaxed with every thought ... allowing yourself to journey inward." Pause.

2. "Imagine that you are walking down a path ... experiencing the sights ... sounds ... feelings ... and smells all around you." Pause. "Enjoying the walk, you begin to notice your body filling with a sense of excitement once again as you look ahead, down the path leading to the large walled city."

3. "The wall is so tall that you cannot see over it. Your eyes search out the eagle atop the immense gate ... an entrance to what lies beyond the wall. You feel eager to explore again what you cannot see. As you draw closer, you feel no fear ... only curiosity, and you think the thought that makes you and the eagle one, and again becoming one with the eagle flying over the wall ... to explore what is on the other side."

4. "Knowing that you are safe, the two of you feel the power of your wings as you soar through the air, seeing your school, home, and neighborhood. Once again, you take this rare opportunity to see your life through new eyes ... without fear ... and without judgment."

5. "Gliding on the winds of change, you can see yourself ... in your future life ... behaving in ways that *are helpful to you and to others* ... feeling the joy and abundance you have created through your behavior changes." Pause.

6. "Take a moment, which is all the time you need, to observe yourself ... living your future ... with family ... with friends ... with authority figures ... at home ... at school ... wherever you may be." Pause one minute.

7. "Having taken a safe, honest look at good, positive changes make your life ... you return to the ground ... just outside the gate. Thanking the eagle for the clear vision ... you walk back up the path, moving your attention to the outside surface of your body ... the air on your face, the pressure of your body against the seat, feeling relaxed and alert ... your eyes, being fully present and ready to work." Pause.

8. "Take one minute to write or draw about another helpful change you see yourself making." Pause one minute. "Put your journals away. "You may speak to the group."

Verification of Participants' Understanding: Review with participants their entries of harmful behaviors and the appropriate needed changes.

Reinforce with Independent Activity: Write a "My Contract for Change" with yourself (see appendix).

Other Resources:
Lusk, Julie T. 1992. *30 Scripts for Relaxation, Imagery and Inner Healing.* Duluth: Whole Person Associates.

Additional Notes:

CREATING SUCCESS

An aim in life is the only fortune worth the finding; and it is not to be found in foreign lands, but in the heart itself.

—Robert Louis Stevenson

Lesson 17: Setting Goals

Grade Level: 6–12-plus

Note: This lesson has four guided imagery activities and is best done in two to four sessions.

Purpose and Overview: Most of us have dreams of how we would choose our lives to be, what we would like to do—pass math, get a date for the dance, go to college, become a professional athlete, travel to foreign countries. We have dreams of relationships—getting along with family and having love and respect from others, many friends. We have dreams of a lifestyle—living in a nice neighborhood or a beautiful home, driving a new car, having money to buy things we cannot afford now, or using our talents to help others less fortunate. Many of us do not realize the power we have to make our dreams come true or the role our imaginations play in this process. Olympic athletes in Chula Vista, California, know that harnessing their mental potential often means *previsualizing* success. There are reasons that visualization produces results:

- Everything in the universe is an energy vibration making us an inseparable part of this universe. Everything is interconnected. We see differences because each object has a different wavelength and density.
- Our thoughts are measurable energy fields projected into the whole and influencing the outcome of the universal creativity. Each thought, action, and event is connected and influences each other. Since everything is connected, the outcome connects to our thoughts.
- By repeating the same thought, the subconscious mind drives us to act on it. In this way, habits are established.

- Each thought we think arouses an emotion. When strong emotions energize a thought, more energetic and definite action follows. Such an action brings results in accordance with the thought that prompted it. When one person has a need and another person can fill it, their thinking, if strong enough, can bring them together.
- Combining imagination and visualization with a concrete goal-setting process helps participants become more successful in their lives.

Objective: The participants will be able to conceptualize the process of goal setting as a necessary step in achieving a desired outcome.

Materials Needed:
1. Imagery script or Grand Ideas from Within Counselor Edition, Volume 4, track 4, "Visualizing Success" (6:22); track 5, "Specific Intent" (6:04); track 6, "Acting Successfully" (6:34); track 7, "Accomplishments" (6:46)
2. Display of weekly title and quote
3. Writing and drawing tools
4. A copy of the "Goal-Setting Worksheet" (see appendix)

Present Lesson Overview and read or play imagery activities:
Imagery Script:

Visualizing Success

Volume 4, track 4 (6:22)

Day 1: Participants remain seated with relaxing music playing in the background.

1. Say, "Do not speak until directed. As you breathe in and out through your nose … closing your eyes, allow my voice to guide you … as all … other … sounds … fall into the background. You know you have complete control over your imagination and are free to go wherever you like within your own mind. Becoming more relaxed … move your attention from the outside surface of your body … the air on your face … to your relaxing muscles." Pause. "Feeling more relaxed with every thought … allow yourself to journey inward." Pause.
2. "Imagine that you are walking through a light fog along a path of stepping-stones. The air is cool … moist … still … and silent. Even though the fog is light, you have to focus on your footing to avoid stumbling or falling … and just ahead of you … the fog lifts … allowing you to see a flight of golden stairs … leading into the clouds. Pause.

"Standing at the bottom of the stairs is the protector ... the one who protects and guides you ... the one who helps make your dreams come true." Pause.

3. "You are eager to climb the stairs ... to see where they lead ... The protector raises a hand ... understanding your eagerness to explore ... yet wanting you to know before you begin that the stairs go *everywhere* ... and *nowhere* ... and that they will only lead *somewhere* with *your* thought and action. The protector asks you to pause and look at the stairs ... disappearing into the clouds ... and to think of where you would like those stairs to lead ... what you would like to achieve when you reach the top." Pause. "Perhaps you would like to stop biting your nails, master a video game, improve your grade on the next math test, or save enough money for an item or activity you want. Pause. "Just imagine something you would like to accomplish ... a challenge ... like those tall golden steps before you ... a challenge you can meet if you carefully climb one step at a time. Whatever your specific goal is, picture the scenario and see yourself acting successfully. Take a minute, which is all the time you need, to choose a worthy goal for yourself." Pause one minute.

4. "The protector kindly suggests that you return tomorrow ... when you may be clearer about what you wish to find at the top of the stairs, and reminds you to *visualize success to achieve success*. Smiling goodbye to the protector ... and knowing you will return ... you walk back up the path, moving your attention to the outside surface of your body ... the air on your face ... and the pressure of your body against the seat, feeling relaxed and alert." Pause. "Open your eyes, being fully present and ready to work." Pause.

5. "Take a minute to write two goals you would like to reach in a week or two and then circle the one you would most like to accomplish." Pause one minute. "Put your journals away. You may speak to the group."

Day 2: Participants remain seated with relaxing music playing in the background.

Imagery Script:

Specific Intent
Volume 4, track 5 (6:04)

1. Say, "Do not speak until directed. As you breathe in and out through your nose ... closing your eyes, allow my voice to guide you ... as all ... other ... sounds ... fall into the background. You know you have complete control over your imagination and are free to go wherever you like within your own mind. Becoming more relaxed ... move your attention from the outside surface of your body ... the air on your face ... to your

relaxing muscles … feeling more relaxed with every thought … allowing yourself to journey inward … and finding yourself once more on the path in the fog."

2. "The fog begins to lift … allowing you to see the flight of golden stairs … leading into the clouds. Standing at the bottom of the stairs once again is the protector … the one who protects and guides you … the one who helps dreams come true."

3. "You are eager to climb the stairs … to see where they lead … as the protector reminds you that the stairs lead *everywhere* and *nowhere* and that they will only lead *somewhere* with *your* thought and action. The protector asks you to pause and look at the stairs … disappearing into the clouds … and to imagine yourself already there, basking in the sunlight of what you have accomplished."

4. "You are unsure, though, of how you get to the top. As you stand at the first step … looking up … you realize that the steps are steep … taller than you realized. The protector helps you onto the first step … the step of *specific intention*."

5. On this step, you must use your mind to describe with as much detail as possible … what you wish to accomplish … choosing something that will require energy to accomplish … yet something that is possible for you to do." Pause.

6. "Choose a length of time you think it will take you to accomplish your goal … and decide *how* you will know when you have reached it. Now looking into the protector's eyes … state your goal." Pause. "The protector smiles … and reminds you to *visualize success in order to achieve success*." Pause.

7. "Now moving your attention from the outside surface of your body … the air on your face … and the pressure of your body against the seat, feeling relaxed and alert … open your eyes, being fully present and ready to work." Pause.

8. "Take a minute to write about or draw your goal … the steps you take to accomplish it … and those who help along the way." Pause one minute. "Put your journals away. You may speak to the group."

Day 3: Participants remain seated with relaxing music playing in the background.

Imagery Script:

Acting Successful
Volume 4, track 6 (6:34)

1. Say, "Do not speak until directed. As you breathe in and out through your nose … closing your eyes, allow my voice to guide you … as all … other … sounds … fall into the background. You know you have complete control over your imagination and are free to go wherever you like within your own mind. Becoming more relaxed … move

your attention from the outside surface of your body … the air on your face … to your relaxing muscles … feeling more relaxed with every thought … allowing yourself to journey inward." Pause.

2. "You find yourself once more on the path in the fog." Pause. "The fog begins to lift … allowing you to see the flight of golden stairs … leading into the clouds. Waiting at the bottom of the stairs once again is the protector. Moving onto the step of *specific intention*, you clearly recall your goal." Pause.

3. "The protector trusts, as you look up at the golden stairs that disappear into the clouds, that you know where you would like those stairs to lead … what you would like to achieve." Pause.

4. "The protector offers you a hand … assists you to the next step … and directs you to imagine one small thing you need to do to accomplish your goal." Pause. "Perhaps you notice a tingle of excitement as you look ahead and approach something you desire." Pause.

5. "As the protector assists you to the next step, you notice you are standing with all those who want to see you reach your goal … Perhaps you notice friends … family members … pets … or people from your church or school. You pause a moment to enjoy the good feelings … breathing deeply as you take them in and allow the warmth to flow all through your body." Pause.

6. "Realizing how far you have come … and what you have accomplished … you smile goodbye … and move your attention from the outside surface of your body … to the air on your face … and the pressure of your body against the seat … feeling relaxed and alert … Open your eyes, being fully present and ready to work." Pause.

7. "Take a minute to write about or draw your goal, the steps to take to accomplish it, and those who help along the way." Pause one minute. "Put your journals away. You may speak to the group."

Day 4: Participants remain seated with relaxing music playing in the background and a copy of their "Goal-Setting Worksheet."

Imagery Script:

1. Say, "Do not speak until directed. As you breathe in and out through your nose … closing your eyes, allow my voice to guide you … all … other … sounds … fall into the background. You know you have complete control over your imagination and are free to go wherever you like within your own mind. Becoming more relaxed … move your attention from the outside surface of your body … the air on your face … to your

relaxing muscles." Pause. "Feeling more relaxed with every thought ... allow yourself to journey inward." Pause.

2. "And find yourself once more on the path in the fog just as the fog begins to lift ... allowing you to see the flight of golden stairs ... leading into the clouds. You notice the protector is waiting for you. Moving on to the step of *specific intention*, you clearly recall your goal ... the steps you will take to achieve it ... and the people who will support you along the way." Pause. "Perhaps you notice a tingle of excitement as you look ahead ... and approach something you desire."

3. "The protector trusts, as you look up at the golden stairs disappearing into the clouds, that you know where you want those stairs to lead ... what you want to achieve, and magically you find yourself there ... moving into the clouds. You look down ... and realize how far you have come ... and what you have accomplished ... You recognize those who helped along the way ... and you step up ... up into the clouds ... up into your new reality—the reality of having made a dream come true."

4. "You see yourself ... having accomplished what you set out to do ... and you experience how it feels to reach your goal ... the excitement ... the satisfaction ... the joy. Whatever your specific goal, picture the scenario and see yourself acting successfully. Long pause."

5. "You become aware that a beautiful white light surrounds and fills you to the point of almost glowing ... and you know that this feeling will stay with you for quite some time." Pause.

6. "The protector catches your attention. You smile goodbye to one another and this time *you* say, '*Visualize success to achieve success*' ... and moving your attention from the outside surface of your body ... to the air on your face ... and the pressure of your body against the seat ... you can feel relaxed and alert ... Open your eyes, being fully present and ready to work." Pause.

7. "Take a minute to complete your 'Goal-Setting Worksheet.'" Pause one minute. "Place worksheet in your journal and put your journal away. You may speak to the group."

Day 5: Participants remain seated with relaxing music playing in the background.

Imagery Script:

Accomplishments
Volume 4, track 7 (6:46)

1. Say, "Do not speak until directed. As you breathe in and out through your nose ... closing your eyes, allow my voice to guide you ... as all ... other ... sounds ... fall

into the background." Pause. "Becoming more relaxed ... move your attention from the outside surface of your body ... the air on your face ... to your relaxing muscles." Pause. "Feeling more relaxed with every thought, you journey inward." Pause.

2. "Moreover, you find yourself once more on the path in the fog just as the fog begins to lift ... allowing you to see the flight of golden stairs ... leading into the clouds. You notice the protector waiting for you. Moving on to the step of *specific intention*, you clearly recall your goal ... the steps you will take to achieve it ... and the people who will support you along the way." Pause. "Perhaps you notice a tingle of excitement as you look ahead ... and approach something you desire."

3. "The protector trusts that you know, as you look up at the golden stairs disappearing into the clouds, where you would like those stairs to lead ... what you would like to achieve, and magically you find yourself there ... at the top of the stairs ... moving into the clouds. You look down ... and realize how far you have come ... and what you have accomplished. Pause. "You recognize those who helped along the way ... helped you step up ... up into the cloud ... up into your new reality—the reality of having made a dream come true."

4. "You see yourself ... having accomplished what you set out to do ... and you experience how it feels to reach your goal ... the excitement ... the satisfaction ... the joy. Whatever your specific goal, picture the scenario and see yourself acting successfully." Long pause.

5. "You become aware that a beautiful white light surrounds and fills you to the point of almost glowing ... and you know that this feeling will stay with you for quite some time ... and you hear yourself say the words of the author Henry David Thoreau: '*Go confidently in the direction of your dreams. Live the life you have imagined.*' The protector catches your attention ... and you *both* say, '*Visualize success to achieve success.*' You smile goodbye to one another ... and moving your attention from the outside surface of your body ... to the air on your face ... and the pressure of your body against the seat ... you feel relaxed and alert ... Open your eyes, being fully present and ready to work." Pause.

6. "Take a minute to write about or draw your goal, the steps you took to accomplish it and those who helped along the way." Pause one minute. "Put your journals away. You may speak to the group."

Verification of Participants' Understanding: Information in journals relative to a specific goal, steps needed to reach that goal, and an appropriate completion date

Reinforce with Independent Activity:
1. Have participants complete the "Goal-Setting Worksheet."
2. Have participants conduct an experiment to prove that circumstances and events follow thoughts.
3. Have participants take any situation or happening in their lives and go back to find what kinds of thoughts preceded the event, sharing the findings with the group.

Other Resources:

Hopper, Carolyn. 2003 "Five Elements of a Useful Goal." *Practicing College Learning Strategies 3rd Edition*. Boston: Houghton Mifflin.

Additional Notes:

BRIDGES TO THE FUTURE

The best way to predict the future is to invent it.

—Alan Kay

Self-image sets the boundaries of individual accomplishment.

—Maxwell Maltz

Lesson 18: Envisioning the Future

Grade Level: 6–12-plus

Purpose and Overview: Children, teenagers, and even adults give very little thought to their long-term futures. Schoolwork requires some sense of goal setting and planning, as does caring for one's family or succeeding in a profession, yet very few individuals realize that the planning they do today is a means to attaining their dreams thirty or forty years from now. Of course, most of us understand that our life's vision may change over time; however, it is important to begin now to visualize the future we are hoping to create.

For instance, a career in professional sports is unlikely if the participant is not currently playing and showing improvement in the chosen sport. A college degree is unlikely as well unless the participant is currently studying to pass middle and high school core subjects.

Imagining your future is like investing your money. If you invested twenty-five dollars today in an account paying 8 percent interest, and added twenty-five dollars per month, your account would have $14,433.05 at the end of twenty years. Invest an equivalent amount of imagination into your future and you will get big dividends as well—confidence, happiness, success, and fulfillment.

Objective: Participants will be able to improve imagery skills by visualizing the details of desired future outcomes.

Note: This lesson may be completed in one or two sittings, depending on the age of participants.

Materials Needed:
1. Imagery script or Grand Ideas from Within Counselor Edition: Audio-Guided Imagery, Volume 4, track 8, "My Future Life" (7:26)
2. A copy of "My Future Life" worksheet (see appendix)
3. Writing or drawing materials

Present Lesson Overview:
Read imagery script or play audio, Volume 4, track 8 (7:26).

Imagery Script:

My Future Life in Ten Years

Volume 4, track 8 (7:26)

Day 1: Participants remain seated with relaxing music playing in the background and a copy of the first page of "My Future Life" handout.

1. Say, "Do not speak until directed. As you breathe in and out through your nose … closing your eyes, allow my voice to guide you … as all other … sounds … fall into the background. Becoming more relaxed … move your attention from the outside surface of your body … the air on your face … to your relaxing muscles." Pause. "Feeling more relaxed with every thought … allow yourself to journey inward." Pause.

2. "Imagine yourself in your room at home. A strange noise draws your attention outside." Pause. "You look out the window and see an unusual contraption resembling a spaceship. You rush outside to investigate … and as you climb on board and look at the instrument panel … you realize you are inside a time machine. You take a seat and strap yourself in."

3. "Filled with excitement and uncertainty, you push the button next to the words *ten years*. There is a loud noise and a bright flash as the capsule goes dark. Almost instantly, you hear and feel a *thud* just as the lights return … and you open the door to see what happened." Pause.

4. "As you step outside, you realize that what you see is both familiar and unfamiliar. Looking around, you realize that you have stepped into the future … your future … your life … ten years from now. You mentally figure out how old you are … and you begin to notice the details of this … your future life." Pause.

5. "You watch yourself go through a day of your future. You see yourself in the house where you live … and you see who is there with you … perhaps a pet … or friend … a roommate … or family member." Pause.

6. "You watch yourself leave the house … wondering where you are going and observing how you get there." Pause. "And now you know where you were going and are seeing what you do … and hearing with whom you interact … and feeling, smelling, and tasting this future moment." Pause. "Curiously living the life that is yours in the future, the life you desired in your past … in the then and there … happening here and now … *that* time and place in *this* time and place." Pause one minute.

7. "As the day ends … you return to the space module once more. You step inside … take your seat … and push the button next to the words *return to present*. Once again, there is a loud noise and a bright flash as the capsule goes dark. Almost instantly, you hear and feel a *thud*, and just as before, the lights return … and you step outside the capsule to find yourself in the present." Pause. "Moving your attention to the outside surface of your body … the air on your face … and the pressure of your body against the seat, back in this room, you feel relaxed and alert … Open your eyes, being present and ready to work." Pause.

8. "Take a minute to complete the *ten*-year portion of 'My Future Life' worksheet." Pause one minute.

Imagery Script:

My Future Life in Twenty Years

Day 2: Participants remain seated with relaxing music playing in the background and a copy of the twenty-year "My Future Life" worksheet.

1. Say, "Do not speak until directed. As you breathe in and out through your nose … closing your eyes, allow my voice to guide you … as all other … sounds … fall into the background. Becoming more relaxed … move your attention from the outside surface of your body … the air on your face … to your relaxing muscles." Pause. "Feeling more relaxed with every thought, allow yourself to journey inward." Pause.

2. "Imagine yourself in your room at home. A strange noise draws your attention outside. You look out the window and see an unusual contraption, resembling a spaceship. You rush outside to investigate … and as you climb on board and look at the instrument panel … you realize you are inside a time machine. You take a seat and strap yourself in."

3.   "Filled with excitement and uncertainty, this time you push the *ten-year* button twice. There is a loud noise and a bright flash as the capsule goes dark. Almost instantly, you hear and feel a *thud* just as the lights return ... and you open the door to see what happened.

4.   "As you step outside, you realize that what you see is both familiar and unfamiliar. Looking around, you know that you are stepping into the future ... your life twenty years from now. You mentally figure out how old you are ... and you begin to notice the details of this future life." Pause.

5.   "Somehow, you are able to watch yourself go through another day of your future. You see yourself in the house where you live ... and you see who is there with you." Pause.

6.   "You watch yourself leave the house ... wondering where you are going this time and observe how you get there." Pause. "And now you know where you were going and are seeing what you do ... and hearing with whom you interact ... and feeling, smelling, and tasting this future moment twenty years hence."

7.   "Curiously living the life that is yours in the future, the life you desired in your past ... in the then and there, happening here and now, that time and place in this time and place." Pause one minute.

8.   "As the day ends ... you return to the space module once more. You step inside ... take your seat ... and push the button next to the words *return to present*. Once again, there is a loud noise and a bright flash as the capsule goes dark."

9.   "Almost instantly, you hear and feel a *thud* ... and just as before, the lights return ... and you step outside the capsule to find yourself. Move your attention to the outside surface of your body [pause], the air on your face ... and the pressure of your body against the seat, back in this room, feeling relaxed and alert ... opening your eyes, being present and ready to work." Pause.

10. "Take a minute to complete the *twenty-year* portion of the 'My Future Life' worksheet." Pause one minute. "Put your worksheet in your journal and then put your journal away. You may speak to the group."

Verification of Participants' Understanding: Participants' worksheet entries describing the time segment indicated in the guided imagery.

Reinforce with Independent Activity: Discuss with participants how the decisions they are making on a daily basis, and the work they are doing in school or community today, are influencing their lives as much as twenty years from now.

SELF-TRANSCENDENCE

MORE THAN THE SELF, MORE THAN THE BODY

There is in you something that waits and listens for the sound of the genuine in yourself. It is the only true guide you will ever have.

—Howard Thurman

Self-transcendence is at the top of Maslow's ladder. Here we use all the skills we acquired from each of the previous steps. On this rung, we feel as if we have one foot on the ground and the other on the stars, as though we are in another dimension—the fifth dimension, the space of the soul. I welcome you here with much love. Dream your dreams and enjoy living them.

Thank you for allowing us to accompany you on this intimate and courageous journey within yourself, a life time adventure.

APPENDIX

COMMUNICATION DIAGRAM

(Input: listening)

I. External Events:

Sensory input through our five senses: *V, A, K, O, G*

(Encode: translate)

II. Internal Processing Filters:

Determines how information is deleted/distorted to generalize the following:

    A. Meta Programs
        1) Internal process (*how* we think)
        2) Internal state (*what* we feel)
    B. Attitudes: Values and Beliefs
    C. Memories
        1) Representation of time
        2) Conscious/unconscious decisions

III. Universal Modeling Process:

The mind holds only seven, plus or minus two, items of information. We do the following:

    A. *Eliminate* sensory information (*V, A, K, O, G*), shifting background/foreground (for example, comparative deletion), an unspecified verb, no referential index, nominalization)

    B. *Distort* by misrepresenting reality (aids in motivation)—mind reading, lost performatives, complex equivalence, cause/effect

    C. *Generalize* by creating an internal representation–universal qualifier, modal operators

(Decode)

IV. Internal Representation: internal images (output)

V. Language Representation: words representing the images

© 1986, 2009, 2011, 2020 Janice McDermott

MANAGING MY BODY

1. My muscle group that is hardest to relax is my …
2. When I relax all my muscles, I feel …
3. I get more tense when I …
4. Other than sleeping, I am the most relaxed when I …

On the image below, highlight the area where you are most tense most of the time.

LEARNING TO BREATHE

1. Describe your breathing experience:

2. How is conscious breathing to calm yourself useful?

FOREGROUND/BACKGROUND

(artists unknown)

#1

#2

SHIFTING EMOTIONS

Check the ones that are true for your internal image:

Image 1 Limiting	Image 2 No Difference	Image 3 Enhancing
Color or	Color or	Color or
Black and white	Black and white	Black and white
Near or	Near or	Near or
Far	Far	Far
Moving or	Moving or	Moving or
Still	Still	Still
You are in it or	You are in it or	You are in it or
You are out of it.	You are out of it.	You are out of it.

© 2004, 2011, 2020, Janice McDermott

MY HOUSE OF MIND

Who are the people living in each category 0f your "House of Mind"? (You can have several in each category.)

1. Mentor:
2. Critic:
3. Nurture:
4. Child:

Draw and label the four shapes in your "House of Mind."

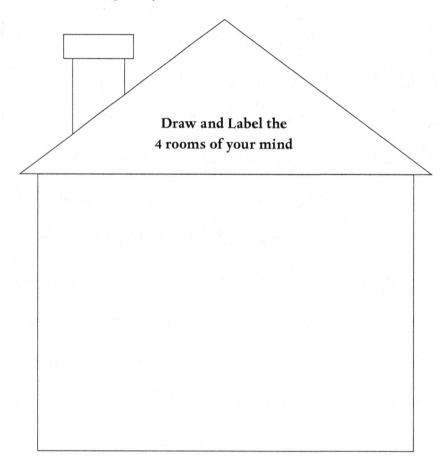

**Draw and Label the
4 rooms of your mind**

ROOMS OF THE MIND CHARACTERISTICS

Mentor (rectangle):
1. Stores (computer-like) time, sequence of events, and experiences
2. None motional
3. Contains factual data
4. Contains accumulated beliefs and values (even when contradictory)
5. Knows the positive intent of other dialoguing parts
6. Constructive

Critic (square):
1. Incapable of love
2. Guiltless
3. Can appear suddenly
4. Attempts to gain recognition, remain important
5. Eavesdrops and interrupts other mental processes
6. Destructive: creates personal suffering, illusion of separateness and despair

Nurturer (heart):
1. Buffers the effects of the critic
2. Unconditionally loving, even to the critic
3. Peaceful, forgiving
4. Nonjudgmental, accepting, validating
5. Intuitive, creative
6. Protective, instructive
7. Purposeful

Child (star):
1. Ceaselessly creative
2. Finds a sense of value present in everything
3. Spontaneous
4. Source of all basic emotions
5. Eternally connected to the nonphysical

©1989, 2004, 2011, 2020 Janice McDermott

OBSERVING MY MIND QUESTIONNAIRE

Answer the following questions after each session:

Session 1: The Mentor:

How can you tell in your body when you are in your *mentor* mind?

Session 2: The Critic:
1. Write the sentence you hear in the room of the critic.

2. Is it male or female?

3. What happens to your body when you listen to this critical voice?

4. Name two significant people who live through their voices or images in the room of your mind called the critic.

5. Name the voice that talks the most or the loudest.

6. What is their favorite thing to say to make you feel smaller, weaker, or dumber?

Session 3: The Nurturer:
1. Write the words you hear in the room of the nurturer.

2. Is the voice male or female?

3. Name two significant people who live through their voices or images in the room of your mind labeled *nurturer*.

4. Which one has the most comforting voice or expression?

5. What happens in your body when you listen to this voice?

6. What is your favorite thing said in this room that makes you bigger, stronger, or more confident?

Session 4: The Child:

Circle one need of the child in your room labeled CHILD:

A. Love   F. Companionship

B. Understanding   G. Information

C. Actively engaged   H. Freedom of imagination

D. Positive attention

E. Security

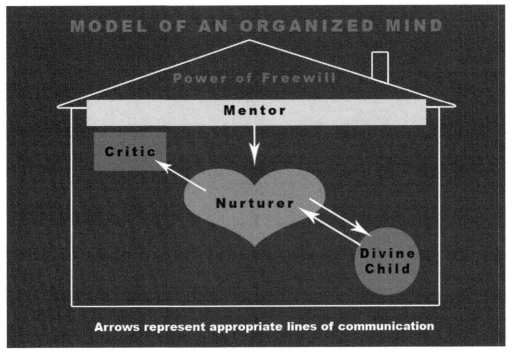

Shapes represent mental categories for sorting thoughts.

Arrows indicate the good form, good function flow for internal dialogues.

LESSON 17 HANDOUT
MY CONTRACT FOR CHANGE

I _____ (name), choose to release the following behaviors that are harmful to me and to replace them with helpful behaviors that will create the future I want.

Release and Replace

| My Negative Behaviors | with | My Positive Behaviors |
| (List) | | (List) |

GOAL-SETTING WORKSHEET

What You Need in Order to Set a Useful Goal:

➢ **Specific Intention:** Describe what you want to accomplish with as much detail as possible—including the date by which you want to accomplish the goal. (For example: "I want to improve my overall grade in Spanish from a B to an A in nine weeks.")

➢ **A Goal That Is Challenging and Possible:** It is possible to bring a subject up one letter grade over nine weeks. It would be unrealistic to expect to do so in one week.

Activities:

I. Write your goal and the date for accomplishing it.

Goal: I choose to:

Date: by __/__/__

II. List steps for accomplishing your goal. I will:

1.

2.

3.

III. Name the people who will help or encourage you to reach your goal:

IV. Describe how you will feel when you reach your goal.

When I reach my goal, I will feel:

MY FUTURE LIFE

Describe your life **ten years** from now:
(Date: __/__/__):

A. Home:

B. Relationships (people and/or pets):

C. Type(s) of transportation:

D. Activities:

School:

Work:

Play:

E. Other observation:

MY FUTURE LIFE

Describe your life **twenty years** from now:
(Date: __/__/__):

A. Home:

B. Relationships (people or pets):

C. Type(s) of transportation:

D. Activities:

School:

Work:

Play:

E. Other observation:

CONTRIBUTING AUTHOR

(LESSONS 4–8, 11, 17–19)

Joan M. Stewart, MSW—certified Daring Way facilitator. Joan received her BA in psychology (1969) and master of social work (1997) with honors from Louisiana State University. She practices as a licensed clinical social worker and conducts therapeutic groups and spiritual retreats. Joan developed and taught etiquette groups for teens, including the Emily Post Summer Camp, at the Breakers Hotel in Palm Beach, Florida, (1982–87); coauthored (as Joan Coles) *Emily Post Talks with Teens about Manners and Etiquette* (HarperCollins, 1985) and *Emily Post's Teen Etiquette* (HarperCollins, 1995); wrote a monthly etiquette column for The Post Institute (1982–1991); and represented them on national multimedia tours.

Please note:

Since becoming a Brené Brown–certified Daring Way facilitator, Joan is no longer accepting clients for individual psychotherapy. However, she is conducting intensive weekend groups as well as half-day groups based on one of Brené Brown's best-selling books—*The Gifts of Imperfection, Daring Greatly, or Rising Strong*—for those individuals willing and ready to challenge themselves to a better future.

Joan Stewart, LCSW
Baton Rouge, LA 70808
Email: jmsmsw@gmail.com

Printed in the United States
by Baker & Taylor Publisher Services